Fifty Years in Sing Sing

Fifty Years in Sing Sing

A Personal Account, 1879–1929

ALFRED CONYES

Edited by
PENELOPE KAY JARRETT

Foreword by
TED CONOVER

excelsior editions

State University of New York Press
Albany, New York

Published by
STATE UNIVERSITY OF NEW YORK PRESS
Albany

© 2015 Penelope K. Jarrett, Pamela Jean Jarrett,
Robert Vincent Jarrett, and Lauren Gail Jarrett

Foreword © Ted Conover

Excelsior Editions is an imprint of State University of New York Press

For information, contact
State University of New York Press
www.sunypress.edu

Production, Laurie D. Searl
Marketing, Fran Keneston

Library of Congress Cataloging-in-Publication Data

Conyes, Alfred, 1852–
    Fifty years in Sing Sing : a personal account, 1879–1929 / Alfred Conyes ; edited
by Penelope Kay Jarrett ; foreword by Ted Conover.
        pages cm
    Includes bibliographical references.
    ISBN 978-1-4384-5422-1 (pbk. : alk. paper)
    ISBN 978-1-4384-5424-5 (ebook)
    1. Conyes, Alfred, 1852– 2. Sing Sing Prison—History. 3. Correctional
personnel—New York (State)—Biography. 4. Prisoners—New York (State)—
History. 5. Corrections—New York (State)—History. I. Jarrett, Penelope Kay,
1954– II. Title.
    HV9468.C66A3 2015
    365'.6092—dc23
    [B]   2014003511

10 9 8 7 6 5 4 3 2 1

*This book is dedicated to the memory of
my great-grandfather, Alfred Conyes,
to the wardens, keepers, and guards he worked with,
to the tens of thousands of prisoners who served time at Sing Sing Prison
during his fifty years of service,
and to Alfred Van Buren, Jr.,
who transcribed the original manuscript dated 1930.*

Contents

Illustrations

Foreword

Guards know the world of prison intimately, yet few have written books. My *Newjack: Guarding Sing Sing* was based on a ten-month passage through that storied institution in the late 1990s, which I sought in order to be able to write about the job; it is a rookie's chronicle.

Alfred Conyes's memoir is at the other end of the experience spectrum—he wore the guard's uniform for more than fifty years, the very definition of veteran. This account of that career, committed to paper by a relative in 1930 and never before published, holds interest in part because it spans so many of the most tumultuous years of American penal history. Conyes was an eyewitness to and participant in practices which are no more: harsh physical punishments such as dangling a prisoner on a peg by his handcuffs; forcing prisoners to work twelve-hour days in prison shops for outside contractors; double-bunking prisoners in cellblocks made of stone, with little fresh air and no plumbing; frequent changes of politically-appointed wardens in the days before prison jobs became "professionalized"; hangings for capital cases in New York, and the frequent use of Sing Sing's electric chair that followed the change to electrocution; and constant attempts at escape, including via the Hudson River.

He was also witness to one of the most daring experiments in American penal history, the prisoner-run Mutual Welfare League, established by the reformer Thomas Mott Osborne during his tenure as warden. And he had the good fortune to spend the last ten of his fifty years in the administration of Lewis Lawes, another famous reformer. Lawes (who, like Conyes, began his prison career as a guard at Clinton Prison in Dannemora, New York) became warden in 1920 and worked tirelessly to keep his prison in the public eye and present his prisoners as human beings, hosting a radio show, appearing on newsreels, inviting major league sports teams to play at the prison (sometimes against inmate teams) and cooperating with Warner Brothers in the production of movies such as *Each Dawn I Die* and *Angels With Dirty Faces*. Lawes wrote several books as well as a brief foreword to the present volume.

Conyes summarizes Sing Sing's remarkable history up to his employment, and he quotes numerous newspaper accounts of famous executions and escapes; the most engaging of these are supplemented by his personal knowledge. He was given a special assignment, for example, to guard Martha M. Place, the first woman to be electrocuted in New York, in the days leading up to her date with the chair. Place had suffocated her stepdaughter, struck her husband on the head with an axe, and attempted suicide all on the same day in 1898. Assigned to do guard duty outside her door, Conyes writes, "I was told to keep a close watch as the time for her execution was drawing near and the warden wanted to be sure that she did not kill herself and 'beat the chair.'"

Conyes angered Place by forbidding her to use a staircase she had exercised on, saying "she could easily have thrown herself down the steps." On the day of her execution, however, she asked whether he could be the one to strap her into the chair. He writes:

> Now, I had seen many men die in the chair but the idea of strapping a woman into it was something different. . . .
>
> Taking her arm, I escorted her down the steps, across the prison yard and into the death house. Behind us walked the warden, two keepers, a woman physician, Mrs. Place's spiritual advisor, the Reverend Dr. Cole of Yonkers, and one of the prison matrons. The doomed woman was at-

tired in a black gown which she had made to wear at an
expected new trial. Having failed to get such a trial, she
asked Governor Roosevelt to commute her sentence to life
imprisonment but the petition was refused. . . .

I quickly attached the electrodes after strapping in her
feet. So great was the modesty in those days that a woman
attendant spread her skirts before Mrs. Place so that the
witnesses could not see her ankle as the electrodes were
put into place against her calf. After strapping her arms
down and tightening the broad belts across her chest, I
stepped back and signaled the warden that all was ready.

The clergyman walked quietly away from the chair
just before the current was turned on. . . . The body
scarcely moved. The prayer book in the woman's left
hand twisted across the wrist and slipped partly out as
the muscles relaxed. Her thin lips simply tightened with
the shock. The matron told me afterward that Mrs.
Place had requested that the prayer book be given to
me. . . . Naturally, it is one of my most prized mementos.

The most valuable parts of this book, to my eye, are the pas-
sages in which Conyes recounts personal incidents that cast light on
what his job was like. It is well-known, for example, that prisoners
during the early years of his tenure had to wear striped uniforms (to
facilitate their capture should they escape) and march between buildings in lockstep, one hand on the shoulder of the man in front, eyes
straight ahead, in silence. But never before have I read an account
of how a guard responded when a prisoner broke that rule. ("I had
overlooked it once in a while because it helped keep up the morale
of the men. As in other cases, they took advantage of this until they
had overdone the privilege, so I told them that there would be no
more talking. One of the men paid no attention and his constant
babbling got on my nerves.") Conyes describes in detail how he
handled that vexing case and the aftermath.

Or supervising 130 prisoners at forced labor in the prison quarry:
what do you do when half of them put down their tools and declare

they're on strike? ("I questioned them as to their motive. They replied that they were not getting sufficient food to enable them to do such hard labor. Inwardly, I agreed with them but I could not allow myself to be interested in what they had to eat.") And you're alone with them?

Or when a boy prisoner, sent to Sing Sing for seven years after cutting another kid in a reformatory, is found weeping on Christmas Eve because he's away from his family and Santa Claus will never find him? ("Just a kid—that's all he was.")

A prison officer's work is all about his daily contact with shunned humanity. But he has other relationships, as well. One wishes Conyes had been expansive enough to tell us something about his home life (Did he have a family? Did he live nearby and walk to work?) or the character of his fellow officers. Doing well at the job requires attention to signals from one's superiors about exactly how things are done—enforcement of rules can vary according to who's in charge, for example, and at Sing Sing the warden in charge changed twenty-three times during Conyes's employment. How did guards and prisoners adjust? In particular, how did they adjust to the earth-shaking reforms of the Mutual Welfare League? Surely many officers must have resisted giving prisoners a degree of self-governance.

The book fascinated me most by demonstrating the clear line that connects Conyes's job to those of today's correctional officers. Then, as now, being a prison guard meant managing not an undifferentiated mass of criminals but rather a series of difficult and often threatening individuals. The best officers—and Conyes was surely one of these—manage the challenge not purely through threats of force but by showing respect and, occasionally, sympathy. They must also, at the core, believe in the efficacy of the system. Time and again Conyes tells how a misbehaving prisoner, initially punished by him, would mend his ways and ultimately thank Conyes for the correction.

One imagines that after fifty years in such a harsh environment a guard would have developed thick skin, and indeed, Conyes leaves some painful things out. We're never told about the longtime executioner, John Hulbert, who killed himself in 1929; mental illness hardly exists in this account of a prison that for years has been a notorious generator of it. We hear almost no details of the perennial corruption that marred prison management in those days, nor of fellow guards doing anything wrong, nor of sexual activity. This is no tell-all. Conyes is a good soldier who never complains—nowhere does he betray that the job ever weighed on him. So it comes as something of a surprise when he writes, at the end, "In consideration of the surroundings, my life has been quite enjoyable, but I doubt if I would ever again go through it. I cannot conceive of a work more weighed down with moral responsibility for . . . hundreds of broken, helpless, imprisoned men. Their welfare is in our hands for long, dreary years."

He struck a more upbeat note ten years earlier in *The New York Times*, in a news item marking his transition from active prisoner management to a tower post overlooking the prison's waterfront. Under the headline "Ends 41 Years in Service: Alfred Conyes Still Active as Sing Sing's Oldest Employee," the old guard is quoted as saying, "I never felt better in my life, and never felt more satisfied." But his book was never published. It is finally seeing the light of day due to the tireless efforts of a great-granddaughter, Penny Jarrett, who, after her mother died in 2008, found the original manuscript "tucked away among her many books" in Florida. Among other effects Alfred Conyes saved there were his hickory billy club—and the little book of scripture given him by Martha M. Place.

Ted Conover
New York City

FIGURE 1. Checkerboard made from stone chips by a prisoner and given to Alfred Conyes. Photo from the Conyes family archives.

Preface

My family visited my grandparents in Ossining, New York, several times a year when I was a young girl. I remember being drawn to the checkerboard in my grandfather's den. My grandfather, Stan Conyes, had an extensive rock collection, drawing boards, easels with paintings in progress, and multiple art books and magazines, but it was the checkerboard that caught my eye, time and time again. I was told the checkerboard had been made by a prisoner at Sing Sing Prison and given to my great-grandfather, Alfred Conyes, when he worked there as a prison guard. I didn't have the opportunity to meet my great-grandfather, but I remember thinking, even as a young girl, that he must have been a good man if a prisoner had handcrafted such a nice gift for him. I knew nothing of prison labor, punishments, or outside contracts and little else about my great-grandfather. I just admired the checkerboard and the connection it provided to my great-grandfather.

In 2008, when my mother, Virginia Conyes Jarrett, passed away, I discovered my great-grandfather's manuscript, *Fifty Years in Sing Sing*, tucked away among her many books. Upon reading it, I realized that my thoughts as a young girl some fifty years ago about the character of my great-grandfather were indeed true. As a prison guard in the late 1800s to early 1900s, carrying out harsh punishment was part of his job. It was a task he disliked, but in his position he had little choice but to do as he was told. He much preferred treating the men with fairness and respect. He realized that a kind gesture on his part went a long way with the prisoners. When prison reform came, he welcomed the changes it brought. Upon retirement from active duty as a prison keeper, Alfred became an official prison guide. Perhaps this is when he told his memoirs to Alfred Van Buren, Jr., who, inspired by their mutual desire to see it published one day, put his words to paper using a manual typewriter. My great grandfather passed away before his memoir could be published, but I am confident he would be very pleased that *Fifty Years In Sing Sing* is now in print (as well as online, which he could never have imagined) and will be read by others a century after his time at Sing Sing.

Penelope Kay Jarrett

Acknowledgments and Editorial Note

I wish to extend my deepest appreciation to Ted Conover for writing the foreword to *Fifty Years in Sing Sing*, as well as for his guidance and encouragement to get the manuscript into publication. Guy Cheli, author of *Images of America—Sing Sing Prison*, has generously shared his expertise and endless enthusiasm about the history of the prison and been instrumental in the acquisition of the photos from Mike DeVall, the Ossining Historical Society, and from his own collection. Joan Jacobsen, daughter of Warden Lewis Lawes, kindly gave her permission to reference in the book the published and unpublished writings of her father. Adam Ace Wolpinsky, fine-art photographer, did an excellent job turning the old and faded group photos into usable images. Author Fred Arment gave valuable suggestions on edits for the book, for which I am also very grateful. My thanks go to the director of Fort Myers Beach Library, Dr. Leroy Homerding, for reviewing the manuscript and providing his professional edits and suggestion to add photos to the book. Beverly Williamson generously retyped the manuscript into a Word document. Friends Betty Leake, Maureen Berger, Sandy Chronis, and Marcy Meadows provided valuable input on the manuscript. Kate, Mary, and Vince Aug gave me encouragement through this new and challenging publication process. My sister, Pam Jarrett, provided the family photos and our great-grandfather's keepsakes pictured in the book. John Gaffney graciously took photographs of several of the collectible items. My sincere appreciation goes to Amanda Lanne-Camilli, Fran Keneston, Laurie Searl, and Jessica Kirschner at SUNY Press for their patience and assistance in bringing Alfred Conyes's book to fruition. Lastly, I wish to thank and lovingly remember my mother, Virginia Conyes Jarrett, for had she not kept the original manuscript throughout several moves, this book would not exist.

Note

Alfred Conyes's manuscript did not include all of the sources for his referenced quotes. Had he lived to submit the manuscript for publication, I am sure he would have given full credit to all of his sources. I have done my best to identify all of the sources that were used in writing his memoir, and extend my sincere apologies for those sources that were not acknowledged. I would like to give credit to Lewis Lawes for his unpublished writings and his book *Life and Death In Sing Sing*. It is evident that Alfred Conyes had a high regard for Warden Lawes and may have used his writings as a resource in writing *Fifty Years in Sing Sing*. Also, Alfred Conyes used the terms *darky* and *Negro* and quotes a prisoner using the language of Uncle Remus. Because these terms were in common use when Alfred Conyes worked in the prison system, I have left them alone despite my personal discomfort; I hope that readers are not offended and will not assume that Alfred Conyes viewed people differently because of the color of their skin.

Foreword

. ◆ —————— ◆ .

1930

Mr. Alfred Conyes holds an enviable record of service. Coming to Sing Sing Prison as a guard, while still a young man, he passed through varied phases of penal policies and experiences. During his fifty-one years of continuous duty, he was a witness to the inhuman oppressiveness of the final decades of the nineteenth century, when men on entering prisons, lost not only their identity, but their minds and health and became the forgotten slaves of an impersonal penal system. He was able to watch the dawn of better days . . . when men learned that oppression and harshness and "solitary" would not bring out the good in men . . . that no matter how fallen or desperate, there was always the spark of hope that could be fanned and encouraged to better things.

Through it all, Mr. Conyes has been able to maintain his genial spirits, his faith in men and a sense of humor that bids well to mellow his years with continued charm and retrospection. We shall all imbibe some of that spirit in turning the pages of the story of his experiences.

Sing Sing Prison,
Lewis E. Lawes,
March 20, 1930
Warden

SING SING STATE PRISONS, 1868.
MALE AND FEMALE

STATISTICS 1866.   Location - at Sing Sing, on east bank Hudson River, 32 miles from New York City.   Established.—Male Prison, in 1825; Female Prison, in 1835.   Area of Prison
Grounds, 71 1/2 acres.   Valuations.—Real, $819,671.50; Personal, $280,434.66; Total, $909,106,16.   Average number of Convicts for the year,—Males, 1193; Females, 144.   Occupation,—Males.
—Upon Contracts for Individuals, 174; For the State, making Chains, 58; Upon Quarries, (producing Building-Marble, Lime, Fluxion and Marble Dust) 235 ; Tailors, Shoemakers, Carpenters,
Laborers, Cooks, &c., 330.   In Hospital, 21; Disabled, 32; Total, Sept. 30, 1868, 1,350.   Females.—Upon Contract, 83; Making and Repairing Convict Clothing and general help, 43 ; In Hospital,
7 ; Total, Sept. 30, 1868, 133.
REFERENCES.—1, Male Prison, 482 feet Long, 42 feet wide, 50 feet high, containing 1191 cells, in six tiers.   2, Female Prison and Matron's Residence, 117 Cells.   3, Agent and Warden's
Residence.   4, Hospital.   5, (1st floor) Kitchen and Dining Hall ; (2d floor,) Chapel and State Shop.   6, Wash, Drying and Bath Rooms.   7, Guard House and Armory. 8 8 8, Cabinet Shops.
9 9, Malleable Iron Shops.   10 10, Shoe Shops,   11 11, Saddlery Hardware Shops.   12, Chain Shop.   13, Marble Dust Mill.   14, Lime Store House. 15 15 15 15, Quarry Railroad.   16, Quarry
Office.   17, Stables.   18, Barn.   19, Clothing Shop.   20 20 20 20 20, Marble Quarries.   21 21 21 21 21, Lime Kilns.   22, Guard Posts.   23 23, Hudson River Rail Road.   24, Depot

FIGURE 2. Sing Sing Prison c.1868. During his fifty years of service, Alfred Conyes worked in many areas, including the stove shop, laundry, shoe shop, and stone shed. Photo courtesy of the Ossining Historical Society.

Prelude

Look up unto the hills whence cometh thy strength.
Look up unto the walls whence cometh despair.

—adaptation of Psalm 121:162

Fifty years behind prison walls as a guard and keeper is an experience which few would choose and still less endure. In my service to the state for over half a century, I have seen many changes in prison administration and discipline. It is clear that modern methods are far more effective than those used in the era of the striped suits, ball and chain, lock-step, and physical torture. I have worked and watched over men from every walk and station in life—rich and poor, high and low, black and white. The majority of these were educated and in many cases professional men including lawyers, doctors, editors, and clergymen. Their imprisonment often prompted me to wonder why people of this class would find their way to prison. Most of them were gentlemen, nice people to know personally and would compare favorably with many on the other side of the wall.

Why someone chooses to commit a crime is, in my opinion, difficult to determine. The reasons, if not the excuses, for their crimes are numerous, but when a man enters upon a career of crime, he may be assured of ending in one place—prison.

FIGURE 3. Alfred Conyes. Photo from Conyes family archives.

Formerly, a prisoner was given a number and thereby, lost his identity. Hope of release was as faint as the light which trickled in through the narrow bars of his cell. Now, at least, the prisoner can cling to his identity and hold on to his hope for an ultimate and timely release. To deprive him of his name and all hope of release is more severe than one might imagine.

People may wonder why convicts are not simply locked up in their cells and then kept there all the time. Running a prison would be greatly facilitated by this method. The main reason why this is not done is because these same men will someday return to the outside world. They have fallen far enough from grace when they enter prison. Why kick them down still more? Prisons are not only places for punishment, but also for correction and training. The general belief is that punishment is supposed to reform the criminal, to protect society, and to deter others. However, punishment is nothing but a way in which we "get even" with the criminal. If we drop this attitude and encourage the inmates in the better things of life, they are more apt to form better ideals and endeavor to lead an honest, wholesome life after their dismissal from the institution. If they are knocked about by brutal guards and threatened with various tortures, they come to believe, "What's the use?" and let it go at that. Brute force has never reformed any man. Prisoners cannot be made to change their manner of living. They must be shown. The main object of prisons and prison officials is to make law-abiding men out of those who have previously broken the statutes. The task is not easy, but neither is it hopeless.

Through all my years as a prison guard, I have kept the belief that there is a great deal of useful material to be found in the "rubbish pile" of humanity behind prison walls. The social structure of a criminal or convict may be entirely rebuilt if only the rough spots are leveled off and straightened up. No man is totally bad. I have been associated with more than 60,000 prison inmates, and somewhere in these men is a vital spark, which if encouraged in the proper channels, will aid in their future development and reform.

Destiny Carved in Stone

· ◆ · ────── · ◆ ·

I was born in the village of Plattekill, New York, on May 29, 1852. Plattekill is situated in Ulster County about ten miles north of Kingston. The neighborhood sits between the Plattekill and Esopus Creeks, in the south part of the town of Saugerties. The Reformed Church, parsonage, schoolhouse, and cemetery are in the nearby vicinity.

The foothills of the mountains where I was born were rich in bluestone. This stone was considered a luxury, if not a necessity, fifty years ago for the construction of buildings. Sidewalks, curbing, and window casements all afforded a constant demand for bluestone, to say nothing of the foundations which were constructed from the rubbish left in the quarries. The piers of the Brooklyn Bridge were taken from the quarries of those mountains. Who cannot recall the beautiful pieces of great bluestone which surround the Vanderbilt mansion at the corner of 5th Avenue and 59th Street in New York City? They are a work of art and excite the admiration of thousands of passers-by. The casual observer, however, would not and could not realize the amount of hard work required in tenderly removing these stones from their natural bed in the soil and transporting them to where they will be used.

Working in the quarries was no easy task. It required muscle and brawn to extract the stone in addition to a keen eye and a sure stroke to use the chisel and sledge. The hours were long and the pay small. Yet, one could see the results of their work. Therefore, the rivalries of the stone cutters became quite intense and partook in what today would be recognized as sport. Quarry gangs would wander from one quarry to another. The life of these people became rugged and rough. When the snows of winter made it impossible to quarry stone because of the intense cold, the gangs would "quarry" ice.

My father, Jacob Conyes, owned thirty acres of quarry land. The stone taken from this property was regarded as the finest quality in New York State. The leading industries were farming and fruit growing, but stone cutting was rapidly forging to the front. A large quantity of the stone used in the construction of the State Capitol

The New York State Capitol.   Albany, N. Y.

Figure 4. Bluestone quarried from land owned by Alfred Conyes's father and stone quarried by prisoners from Sing Sing Prison were used to build the State Capitol in Albany. Photo courtesy of the New York State Library.

at Albany was quarried on my father's land. He would allow men to settle on his farm with the stipulation they pay him a certain amount for every foot of stone quarried on the property. This arrangement provided him a comfortable income. Hence, my father became a man of influence in the community.

A few years after my birth, the name Plattekill was changed to Mount Marion, New York, after the daughter of a prominent farmer. The village has retained this name ever since. I went to school in the village and had my share of chores and odd jobs on my father's farm. Soon, I became strong and old enough to take up stone work. This work appealed to me for I had been brought up in just such an atmosphere. Consequently, most of my early life was spent in quarrying and cutting stone, breaking off the rough edges and preparing them for building purposes. I little dreamed this experience would prove so valuable to me during my career among criminals, who were often the most desperate and violent characters in our penal institutions. Memories of my quarry days would come back to me in the building of the stone walls of Sing Sing Prison intended to isolate men from the rest of the world and forbid all contact with their fellow beings.

As a young man, I wandered from place to place with the quarry gangs learning the trade. Even in stone cutting, an apprenticeship must be served. My apprenticeship was difficult, but I soon became quite proficient at the work. I enjoyed the surrounds of a stone cutter's life and might still have been swinging a sledge had I not become acquainted with a fortune teller who was indirectly responsible for the turn in my life which led me to prison work.

Back in 1877, most of the traveling was done by stage coach. I rode the stage coach to the quarries everyday. Since the ride was slow and tedious, it was only natural that the passengers would pass the time talking and joking. Consequently, I met a woman fortune teller, who later proved to be somewhat of an excellent harbinger, so far as my future was concerned.

The Brown Hotel in Kingston was at that time one of the most popular in the Hudson Valley. Since it was also the terminal of the stage coach lines, many people including stone cutters made the hotel their headquarters when in town. When we arrived, the woman insisted I accompany her into the lobby to have my palm read. I was in a hurry, but there was no polite way out. She prophesied many good things for me—those people generally do. One thing she said remained indelibly impressed upon my mind: "You are a loyal worker, young man. You should be doing something else. Be a boss, for I see signs of great power over men, if you will only bring it out in yourself."

Her words of flattery pleased me greatly. I agreed with her and said I would very much like to be a boss over men. Who wouldn't at that age? The idea kept turning over in my mind and the more I thought about it, the better I liked it. The thought soon became an obsession. After those words of "wisdom," I knew I would not rest until I had found a suitable position. Still, where I might find the place and how to go about it was no small dilemma. A friend unknowingly suggested a solution.

While riding to work one morning, I was delighted to see one of my boyhood chums get on the stage coach. He saw me at once and during the ride we talked of many past experiences. I told him of my audience at the hotel and asked if he could offer any suggestions. Jokingly, he replied that the best place for a boss was in a prison as far as he was concerned. We both laughed. Still, perhaps prison was a good place to be a boss. I became intensely enthusiastic over what had started as a joke. My friend tried to dissuade me, but I was determined to find a position in one of the prisons. Fully convinced my intentions were serious, he promised to introduce me to a keeper at the Sing Sing State Penitentiary.

Sure enough, a few days later I received a caller. He introduced himself as John Hornbeck and told me many things about prison life. I listened attentively asking many questions. He was very kind and our meeting was a pleasant one. I was advised not to enter into this field unless I was certain that I really wanted such a position.

For several days, I carefully went over every detail weighing the good points with the bad. Quarrying was all right, but the prospect of handling convicts fascinated me. The job was surely worth a trial anyway. My main problem would be in obtaining an appointment.

In 1829, to reward his supporters for their political services, President Andrew Jackson introduced a system of handing out appointments to office. Senator Marcy, in a bitter speech against this practice, stated that "to the victor belong the spoils of the enemy." This phrase rapidly became the accepted practice of political action in the country. So well adapted did this practice prove itself to the American party system, it became prevalent in the entire public life of the country. It is interesting to note that in the forty years from the beginning of Washington's administration to that of Jackson, not a single subordinate was removed from office without due cause. During Jackson's first term, such removals numbered well into the thousands.

This new system caused many vigorous and bitter debates in the United States Senate. However, nothing could turn the tide. For more than forty years, no president ever raised his voice against it. Finally, in 1867, the sentiment in favor of reform found expression in a report to the House made by Mr. Thomas A. Jenckes of Rhode Island. This report suggested the establishment of a merit system based upon competitive examinations. Mr. Jenckes made another report in the following year, but Congress failed to take any action until 1871. Then, the first Civil Service Commission was appointed by President Grant. Meanwhile, the politicians were making their own plans and succeeded in having Congress withhold the necessary yearly appropriation for this committee. President Grant yielded and suspended operation of the Civil Service Rules in 1875.

In May 1877, the year I decided to seek my appointment, the Civil Service Reform Association was organized in New York. The Association instituted an active propaganda to generate public sentiment in favor of reform. Speeches and huge mass meetings aided the movement, and the organization became very influential. However, not until July 1883 when Senator Pendleton of Ohio introduced a bill, which passed in both houses of Congress by overwhelming majorities, did the Civil Service Law go into effect. The law "prohibited the vicious practice of levying assessments for partisan purposes upon members of the civil service of the government, authorized the appointment of a commission to frame rules and regulations for the civil service and empowered the president, from time to time, to determine by executive order, what classes of the public services should come under the operations of such rules."[1]

In 1877, obtaining a civil service position was considered quite an accomplishment because the government was in a constant turmoil over how positions were assigned or denied. There was not a single employee in this branch of work who felt assured of his job. Thousands of men were turned out of their positions whenever a new administration went into office; their efficiency was immaterial. Jubilant at being elected, almost every official appointed a friend to a position of high salary with the express agreement that the man was to do no work, whatsoever. Such cases were common and "breaking in" was the most difficult thing in the world. I had very few friends in politics, but those I did have were men of influence.

The Surrogate of Ulster County, Alton D. Parker, granted me an interview and after listening to my plans, agreed to do what he could. Next, I wrote to John D. Schoonmaker, who was New York Attorney General at the time. After some delay, I received a most gratifying reply. Mr. Schoonmaker had managed to interest several state senators in my application. For some reason unbeknownst to me, they wrote and told me that they would do everything in their power to help me. I think Mr. Schoonmaker must have done some "tall" talking. There was nothing more for me to do. I had left no stone unturned to secure my appointment. If I failed now, there was no help for it, and I would have to go back to the quarries. Senators, as a rule, paid little attention to requests such as mine. I could only hope for the best.

It was not long in coming. A few weeks after the first letter from Mr. Schoonmaker, I received another enclosing letters from his friends in the State Senate. Their letters were splendid recommendations to Warden Isaiah Fuller of Clinton Prison and expressed their best wishes for my future success in penal work.

I was pleased, of course, but decided to wait until I had definitely been accepted by the Warden before congratulating myself. Letters of recommendation can sometimes mean very little. Past disappointments had made me somewhat cautious. I would feel better when I drew my first pay check.

I prepared to leave home at once. Plattekill was so small that all of the residents knew each other by sight. Saying farewell was but a matter of an hour or so. Throwing my few belongings into a suitcase, I left for Kingston, where I boarded a train for Albany, and thence to Dannemora, home of Clinton Prison.

Dannemora is a village in Clinton County, northeastern New York, situated about twelve miles west of Plattsburg. The population in 1877 was a shade over two thousand people. There was not much to the place with the exception of the prison.

The construction of Clinton Prison was begun in 1844. At the time of my entrance, the prison consisted of a number of buildings enclosed within a stockade which surrounded thirty-seven acres of land. This particular site had been chosen so the convicts might be employed in the mining and manufacturing of iron. There was an abundance of iron ore on the tract belonging to the prison. The surrounding region was densely wooded and the timber furnished the charcoal used in the furnaces. One thing could be said of the prison commission—they knew a good site when they saw one.

As I walked up the main and only street in the village, I paused occasionally to look over the surroundings. There was very little to see—just a few stores and hitching posts. I was looking for someone who might direct me to the prison. Seeing no one in the street, I entered a store and asked the proprietor. He stared at me without speaking. It was not a very cheery reception. I repeated my question and he nodded his head, pointing with his pipe.

I started up the street once again and after walking about a mile, saw the gates of the prison in the distance. I stopped again, wondering if I had made a mistake, after all. Strange to say, my biggest inspiration at that moment was the prediction of the fortune teller back in Kingston. I had doubted her before, but now her words helped me considerably.

The huge gates swung open to admit me. As they closed, leaving me within the prison walls, I experienced a tightening in my throat, a feeling somewhat akin to being homesick, but it lasted only a moment. I recovered my composure and asked for the Warden. An attendant led me to the Warden's office, where I was cordially and officially welcomed to Clinton. The Warden glanced over my recommendations and smiled.

"Well, Mr. Conyes, your credentials are in good order. It gives me great pleasure to welcome you here. Believe me, sir, there are few men who ever apply for a job such as you desire."

His last comment did not sound very encouraging, but then I remembered that the type of work I had selected would probably be more or less repulsive to many.

"There has been quite a shortage of keepers and guards," continued the Warden, "and I find it difficult to keep my roster up to quota. It is customary to try out newcomers as guards until they prove their ability. However, I think I'll take the chance and make you a keeper. What do you say?"

My reply was quite obvious. Of course, I'd take the keeper's post. The job was not only a better one, but meant ten dollars more a month than I had expected. This last bit of good news was the best of all. I entered the life of a keeper at Clinton full of faith and confidence in my ability to do the new work.

Clinton Prison

· ◆ ———— ◆ ·

An Inside Portrait

During our conversation, short as it was, I learned that the warden was a man of quick action and strong will. He fulfilled all my expectations of what a prison warden should be. I was impressed by both his speech and his physical appearance. The very presence of this man radiated strength. I knew I was going to like him and inwardly hoped that we would get along well together. As we clasped hands at the end of the interview, I knew that I already had one friend in this place for the correction and punishment of those who had done wrong.

There were eighteen hundred inmates in Clinton at this time. They were criminals of the most desperate type. To this day, the worst convicts are sent to Clinton. When a man shows signs of rebellion, all we have to do is mention sending him to Clinton. That is enough, for the men fear Clinton Prison more than anything else. The average age then was about thirty-two years old as compared to that of twenty-three today. The older felons usually offered more resistance and would attempt anything to escape or ease the burden of punishment inflicted upon them by the state. Keeping any number of them in order was to be no easy task. Of this, I was certain. Mr. Hornbeck had given me some good advice in this matter. He knew from experience. The only way to keep the men under control was to impress them with the fact that they were to do as they were

FIGURE 5. Clinton Prison c. 1860–1870 showing the men in striped suits and walking in lock-step fashion. Photo courtesy of Guy Cheli.

told—that I was indeed the boss. The men, I had been told, were quick to take advantage of opportunities however slight or dangerous they might be.

Life in Clinton Prison was in direct contrast to what I had been accustomed to in my former pursuits. Gone were the mountains and hills. In their place were the man-made walls of the prison. Gone was the happy, carefree atmosphere of the country. A feeling of despair and loneliness pervaded my initial impression. I was deeply moved by the surroundings and prisoners over whom I must keep such a close watch. It seemed a pity my fellow men should be penned up in a place such as this. Sympathy, however, constituted only the smallest part of a keeper's concerns. We had to be stern and at times, cruel. Back then the main purpose of punishment was to break the men down physically and mentally. Many were unable to stand prison life and either went mad or committed suicide. In spite of every precaution taken against it, there were many cases of the latter. Life is a pretty dear thing even to a man in prison. One can well imagine the kind of conditions which would prompt him to end it. At first my feelings of concern were somewhat in favor of the prisoners, but after all, they had been a menace to the public safety. Prison rule then dictated they should and must be punished.

Many stories of prison life had come to me during my life in the quarries. Now, I was in a position to see for myself. I soon learned that these horrific tales were not exaggerated in the slightest. If anything, they had greatly underrated punishment practices and prison life.

The food was bad—very bad. Words cannot adequately describe it. How human beings could eat such stuff and live has remained a mystery to me. Breakfast consisted of some prison hash and milk. This hash was all the word implies, and the very thought of it made some of the men sick to their stomachs. At first, they would refuse to eat, but the old timers knew they would have to eat hash or nothing. The new men soon became aware of this fact and learned even prison fare was better than starving to death. If an inmate did not like the taste, he could pass back his plate for some molasses, which was smeared upon the food to seemingly make it more palatable.

After this meal, the men were marched directly to work in lock-step fashion. The morning was spent in hard labor until the call for dinner. A greasy stew was served in the mess hall, but dinner offered very little respite for the men were immediately marched back to work upon completion of the meal.

For supper, the men did not go to the mess hall. They filed past a "bread rack," which was a set of shelves where some bread and a cup of water were put for each inmate. Taking their own portions as they passed, the men filed directly to their cells. They were securely locked in for the night before being allowed to eat. A short time afterwards, the guards went to each cell collecting the dishes, after which the men were left for the night in the loneliness of their quarters.

Prisoners were attired in striped suits made in the prison tailor shop. In addition, their hair was cut very close to the scalp. Both of these measures were taken as steps against possible escape. The barber at Clinton was an artist of high degree. Anything—numerals, circles, and fantastic patterns—might be cut into a convict's hair. The prisoner was not allowed to specify as to the style of cut desired. This privilege rested with the barber alone. An escaped man had quite a time growing more hair into these bald spots. Then, too, the striped clothes made discovery more probable. Escaped men could rid themselves of the clothes, to be sure, but only when a confederate assisted them by securing new outfits. To prevent escapes, when any work was done outside of the walls, the men were heavily shackled together with balls and chains. Guards armed with repeating rifles constantly hovered about. Consequently, attempts to escape were seldom successful.

The cell block, which is the name applied to the building containing the individual cells, was made entirely of stone. There were no windows in this building. The only ventilation was secured through two doors at the entrances. The walls were almost a foot thick, so escape by breaking through them was practically hopeless.

The cells were arranged in galleries one on top of another. A platform about three feet wide served as a boardwalk above the ground floor. These "holes in the wall" were about three feet wide, seven feet high, and eight feet long—the smallest area in which men have ever been imprisoned in this country. There was barely enough room for a convict to stand when his bed was swung down from the wall for sleeping. During the day, beds were left folded against the wall. The only other article in the cell was a bucket. Plumbing was nothing like it is in these modern times. The men emptied their buckets into an open sewer and then washed them out each morning. The buckets were left to dry until nightfall when the prisoner took his bucket back into his cell. There were no electric lights, so each cell was provided with a kerosene lamp. When a man was locked in, there was little for him to do, but sit and think. The space provided was barely enough for one person. However, incredible as it may seem, there were often times when space necessitated two occupants to a cell, the men sleeping in bunks one over the other.

A great deal has been written and said about older methods of punishment in prisons. Some of these descriptions are true while others tend to be exaggerated. There were many instances when a newspaper reporter, carried away by romanticism and cheap adjectives, filled the minds of others with the worst sort of horrible tales. The actual punishments were severe enough. Without witnessing these disciplinary acts, no one can possibly realize how severe they really were. To say the whole system was a terrible one is putting it mildly. It was ghastly!

The sternest of measures were enforced to preserve order in Clinton. Punishment generally ran over what the word implied before modern methods stepped in with more effective, though milder ways. These punishments were horrible. A prisoner had to complete a specified amount of work daily. If he failed to finish his assignment in time, he was punished accordingly.

When a man was brought up to be disciplined, he was first reported to the Principal Keeper (P. K.). After considering the facts of an individual case, the P. K. would mete out punishment in proportion to the nature of the offense.

"Hanging up" was about the most brutal of all the penalties to which the men were subjected. Strange to say, it was used often and not reserved for only the chronic offenders. First, a nail was driven into the wall. Then, the victim, handcuffed, was literally "hung up" on it. His face was turned to the wall, his arms were stretched high above his head and he was left dangling with his feet just far enough from the floor to prevent resting his toes. It was quite obvious the victim would shout to be taken down. As a rule, he was allowed to hang there for a few moments until the officers had assured themselves his screams were genuine. I have seen men hang there against the wall with blood spurting from their wrists until they fainted from the ordeal. The spectacle was anything but pleasant. Still, even this was not considered sufficient discipline.

Generally, after he had been punished in this manner, the inmate was also thrown into a dungeon. This was simply a solitary cell covered in the front by a heavy sheet of steel. There were no windows, and due to the absence of a bed or a cot of any kind, the inmate had to lie on the cold, clammy stones. Sleep was extremely difficult under these circumstances. The light failed to penetrate the solid door and the person within had no concept of the time of day or of anything connected with the outside. It was impossible for him to see his hand before his face. Not a sound could be heard in this cell other than the constant wailing of the inmate. He was continually alone and was left there for indefinite periods, ranging from a few days to as many weeks. During this time, the only food received was a single slice of bread and a gill of water every twenty-four hours. This was passed to the inmate through a small sliding panel in the door. More often, the bread was simply tossed in upon the floor, in which case the poor fellow could be heard crawling over the stones on his hands and knees endeavoring to locate the scrap of food. The dungeon was an experience prisoners would not soon, if ever, forget.

Flogging was the most common form of punishment. This was done in a most unceremonious manner. The culprit was brought into a room provided for that purpose, stripped of his trousers and tied over a chair, face down. The flogging was administered by the P. K. with a heavy wooden paddle about two inches thick. The inmate was dealt three to fifteen blows. Some of the men stood up very well under this punishment while others went completely to pieces. In connection with this measure, I recall one rather amusing episode which occurred while we were flogging a Negro.

This fellow was a huge man weighing well over two hundred pounds. He had been flogged before, but it never seemed to have any effect upon his later conduct. The offenses committed by this particular inmate were numerous. The P. K. did not relish his job, but he wanted to teach the darky a lesson. The guards did their duty in short order, stripping off his trousers and forcing him over the chair. The P. K. went to work with agility surprising for a man of his age. Ten strokes had been the order, but the P. K. stopped short after the third. We looked at him wondering why he did not continue. Standing with the paddle raised, he pointed to the Negro. The man's bowels had moved! He turned his head so that he might see the P. K. and, upon grinning, said, "Looks like yo' shoah struck oil that time, ole Principal Keepah."

All eyes were on the face of the Principal Keeper. I did my best to keep a straight face. The P. K. tried to preserve his dignity, but finally broke a smile. This gave me courage and I joined in with the others. It was my first smile since I had come to Clinton. The humor of the situation saved the Negro for the balance of his punishment was suspended. Many diverting incidents have occurred during my career since then, but I shall never forget the look on the darky's face as he turned and smiled up at his tormentor.

It was of the utmost necessity to keep the men busy during the day. This was done to occupy their minds so they would have little chance to conceive schemes for mutiny and escape. In actuality, the inmates of Clinton were very well-behaved considering their type. During my entire service at this institution, there was but one successful escape. Many had tried, but their attempts had been thwarted. However, the following fellows managed to get away and the story of their return is a strange one.

Shortly after supper, on a bitter cold evening of March 1878, the nightly check-up revealed three men were missing. Word was flashed through the prison at once as the siren shrieked the alarm. To this day, no one knows how the break was made. The weather was so intensely cold that the men were not followed that night. Snow was falling and the wind howled through the trees. The alarm spread until every village and town within a radius of a hundred miles was on the lookout for the fugitives a short time after the break had occurred. Imagine the surprise of the warden when the men staggered into his office the next morning to give themselves up! They were physical wrecks from their exposure to the elements. In explaining their return, they said the weather was so cold, they were unable to go very far before their limbs became frozen. The thermometer had registered thirty degrees below zero. The escaped men knew they had only one chance in a thousand for a complete getaway. They had heard the prison siren and were aware that everyone would be on watch for them. They discussed their impending fate and reached the conclusion that the only thing to do was to turn back to the only place where they would find shelter—the prison. Sure death awaited them on the outside, so they chose the lesser of two evils and gave themselves up. What did they care for punishment when such a fate was snapping at their heels? As I said before, life is a precious thing, even to convicts.

The runaways were dealt with severely and never again tried to escape. They had learned their lesson. They were released a few years later upon completion of their terms. This time the siren was silent and they went their way with the good wishes of the warden. Now, they would have no fear of "hounding by the police."

~

Naturally enough, all work connected with the prison was done by the inmates.

"They kept the institution in order and carried on all domestic arrangements. In addition, repairs and improvements, such as the construction of new buildings, were often done by inmates under expert direction. However, this did not furnish sufficient employment to keep prisoners continually occupied. For the sake of the convict as well as for the pecuniary returns, it was customary to employ the prisoners in productive enterprises.

"The contract system existed in two forms. In the first, the labor of the convict was furnished to contractors for a fixed sum. The contractors furnished the raw material and machinery for producing the product, and personally directed the labor in the institution. In the second form, the piece price system, the contractor furnished the material and paid a stipulated amount for the finished product. The production of the products was in the hands of the prison officials. The advantage of this form was that it avoided the possibility of trouble coming from the presence in the prison of employers who were not directly responsible to the prison authorities.

The former method was utilized in Clinton and Sing Sing.

"It had many advantages. The industry was managed by experts who could buy and sell to better advantage than could the warden who, presumably, was not so well posted. Moreover, the state was not subject to loss because of gluts in the market or because of official ignorance or duplicity. It furnished steady employment for the prisoners and appreciably reduced the net cost of maintenance."[1]

The contract system has since been abolished mainly because of the competition with free labor. Many prison contractors were getting rich at the expense of the convicts. Outside employers condemned the system on the ground that the cheap labor gave the prison contractor an unfair advantage. Labor unions objected because they felt it had a tendency to reduce wages. Then, too, the contractor was supplied at the prison with factory room, storage facilities, heat, light, and power. He hired the prisoners at the rate of fifty-six cents a day per man while the inmates received but one and a half cents. They virtually became slaves of the contractors. They were employed in the manufacture of shirts, overalls, chairs, boots and shoes, hats, brushes, mats, brooms, and stoves. In addition, there was a great deal of stone monument work done for cemeteries, etc. Later, a bill was passed by the State Legislature abolishing contract labor in the prisons. Now, prisoners manufacture products for the exclusive use of the state, county, or public and municipal institutions. In this way, the state furnishes the materials and conducts all business through its officials. Any profits go to the state and any loss is borne by it. Under this system, the individual prisoner may be employed in such work that benefits his best interest.

This contract labor was in vogue while I was superintending fifty inmates in the hat shop. At that time, the pay for a keeper was seventy-five dollars a month. We certainly earned it. At the time, I was sure any man in the place would have put a knife in my back with the greatest of pleasure. Watching just one of a type such as theirs was bad enough. I had my work cut out for me keeping an eye on all of them.

Inmates are prone to "sound out" a new keeper. Consequently, from the first day, I never relaxed my vigil and rarely, if ever, let them see my back. It was too dangerous. Every now and then, I would grant the men a few small favors. In this manner, I gradually succeeded in making them work better with one main purpose in mind—to get the daily work completed. An inmate is usually more respectful in his attitude toward a keeper if he knows he will receive fair play. Bullying was useless—at least in my case. I found that a helping hand could be used to a better advantage with them. They never abused what small kindnesses I granted them, no doubt for fear that they would lose the privileges gained. As a rule, the men did all that was expected and demanded of them. For two years I had very little trouble in maintaining order in the shop. Of course, there were one or two small "revolts," but most of the days passed quietly. I had succeeded in convincing the men that I too was human and not a "tough guy" without a heart.

Twelve hours each day, except Sundays, throughout the year were spent in the shops. This meant but one day of rest in every seventy-two-hour week of hard labor. There were no ball games or recreation periods such as permitted now. Inmates were allowed to smoke only in their cells. Talking was strictly prohibited. About the only things the keeper said were "Yes" and "No." Believe me, we very rarely said "Yes." If an inmate asked for something, he was generally pretty sure of what the answer would be before he spoke.

The rising bell sounded one hour later than usual on Sundays. Immediately after breakfast, those who wished to attend religious service were marched into the chapel. All others were sent directly to their cells, remaining there until Monday morning. Chapel over, those who had attended filed past the "rack," taking pans of rice and prunes on their way to the cells. The others received their meal from guards who distributed food throughout the cell block and collected dishes after the men had finished eating. There were no radios, of course, not half enough air, and very little to read. Sitting and thinking were about the only forms of recreation. Some sang in their cells, some wrote letters and a few prayed, while others cursed their plight and set about contriving ways and means of escape. Practically the only air and sunlight received was during the lock-steps between the shops and the cells. Prison was no place for a "softy."

During the latter part of my service at Clinton, I enjoyed my work and was quite content, but I wanted to be near my parents, as they were getting along in years. I had not been home for some time and felt that I should be with them more often. Then, too, Sing Sing was considered the model penal institution. My friend John Hornbeck was no longer there, but ever since our meeting my desire to see the place had been great. I felt capable of taking care of myself under any conditions now that I had become accustomed to the life of a keeper. The strange atmosphere of my new surroundings had worn off. Sing Sing was the next step; I began to make arrangements for a transfer.

Warden Fuller gave me a fine letter of recommendation to Warden Brush of Sing Sing. My application for a transfer had been approved; I left Clinton in October of 1879. I was sorry to leave Warden Fuller. He had been very kind to me. Later, he gave up prison work and started a shirt factory in Kingston. Pleased over the prospect of at last serving at Sing Sing, I looked forward to many more years in the service of the state.

Sing Sing Prison—Now and Then

Sing Sing is more than a series of large prison buildings for the detention of those who have violated the laws of the state. Today, Sing Sing is a model twentieth-century penal institution which takes the very dregs of society, purging and refining them with the result that it advances, rather than retards, the upward movement of humanity. The conditions which formerly created in prisoners the feeling of being entombed, useless, and hopeless exiles have been removed. The ideals of respect, industry, efficiency, and cooperation have arisen from the new prison conditions and create a beneficial and lasting impression on the mind of each prisoner.

In order to understand the procedures of prison registration, let's follow the course taken by the convict upon his arrival at Sing Sing. Immediately upon entering the prison ground, the court officer escorts him to the arrival room in the basement of the registration building. Here, he is required to answer about sixty different questions, the answers to which furnish a brief history of the man's life, habits, and the particulars of his crime. This record is filed for future reference.

After his record has been compiled, the man receives a number. Contrary to popular belief, the name is not dropped, but is used along with the number. He is then taken to the tailor's shop, where he is fitted with a suit of prison clothes. The old clothing is destroyed or sent to relatives. He is carefully searched to make sure no drugs or other illicit goods are on his person. After a shower, under the supervision of a guard, who makes sure that the man is thoroughly cleansed, he receives his prison suit consisting of a gray coat and pants, socks, a pair of brogan shoes, rough underwear, and a shirt. The striped prison suits passed out of existence many years ago. It makes no difference whether the suit fits, for the man is not going anywhere.

The newly attired prisoner is taken to the hospital, where he is given a thorough physical examination. A chart is retained showing his condition and this record is kept up-to-date during the entire period of his confinement. A psychiatrist and a psychologist conduct mental examinations and study the character and personality traits of the new prisoner. Other examinations are held in the prison school to determine the level of education and prior accomplishments. The prison chaplains interview the incoming man, offering guidance and support. Last, but not least, the prisoner is taken to the Bertillon Department, where pictures and fingerprints are taken of the prisoner and entered into his file. All of the above tests and interviews are compulsory. The findings are of considerable help in assigning the men to a line of work in which they may best acquit themselves. However, during the early days, the men are kept locked in their cells and only allowed out for meals and examinations. Strange as it may seem, this initial period is looked upon by many prisoners as the most difficult part of their prison term.

After these preliminaries, the new men are invariably assigned to shoveling coal and doing other heavy tasks. Every man must first do his bit in this class of work unless he is physically disabled. There are, of course, many who feel their ability in other lines of work are not being acknowledged and resent this introduction to prison discipline, but influence in Sing Sing is unknown. Following this period of hard labor, the men are generally assigned to tasks in line with their qualifications and ability. In such a large institution and with such a large prison population, there is a job and a place for everyone. Work assignments are made by the P. K., the prison physician, the psychiatrist and the prison schoolteacher. The P. K. considers the general traits of the character while the other officials give their opinions as heads of their respective departments. The chances of showing any favoritism are decidedly small because of the many factors taken into considerations in assigning the prisoner's classification. Then, too, by this method, no man is assigned to work which he is found unable to perform.

> Sing Sing in its operation takes on the aspect and assumes the problems of a community. This community composed at the present time of close to seventeen hundred (now twenty-one hundred) prisoners, makes and repairs its own clothing and shoes; cooks and serves its own food; produces its own light and power; makes its own ice; bakes its own bread; conducts its butcher and grocery shop; nurses its own sick under the direction of physicians, surgeons, pathologists and dentists; handles its own sewage; operates its own laundry; conducts its own school; provides for its own recreation; builds its own walks and roads; maintains and repairs its own buildings; . . . does its own barbering; handles and distributes its own mail after it has been officially censored; operates a small farm and repair garage with its fleet of motor trucks; conducts its own religious exercises under the supervision and direction of specially qualified chaplains whose devotion to their work has caused many a man to have a change of heart; handles its own library; has its own morgue; polices its own grounds and regulates its own traffic; has its own set of laws (rules), a court to try its own offenders, and a "jail within a jail" for them; and, in addition, operates factories that annually produce more than $650,000 worth of products.

FIGURE 6. Recreation yard at Sing Sing c. 1929. Photo courtesy of the Ossining Historical Society.

There are also many different kinds of specialty work done at Sing Sing. A watchmaker is kept busy repairing numerous clocks in offices and shops; a skilled locksmith looks after the thousands of locks, and a key room is operated to monitor and inventory the keys; an expert welder repairs the bars, some of which are occasionally tampered with; a statistician looks after files and compiles various record charts; a publicist assists in the preparation of the catalogue of prison products; an interpreter translates the foreign mail for the censor; an undertaker assists in the autopsies, etc. Plumbing, painting, rock quarrying, stone crushing, concrete work, and machine shop afford employment and skilled trade instruction.

With more than one hundred and fifty different kinds of work to be done, it is not, as a rule, difficult to assign most men to work for which they are somewhat fitted. Among the recent exceptions have been a sky-writing aviator, a deputy jail warden, a radio announcer, a judge, a preacher, a bartender, a pugilist, a masseur, and a pretzel peddler. However, work they must. The sky-writer was given the job of painting the smoke stacks and roofs; the deputy warden was put in charge of the chickens; the radio announcer received a mop; the judge was made a waiter in the mess hall; the preacher was assigned to the daily task of cleaning the chapel; the bartender was put to washing dishes; the pugilist was a firefighter in the power house; the masseur was given the job of manicuring the yard; and the pretzel peddler was assigned to the scavenger cart.[1]

The prisoners are awakened by a gong at 6 A.M. A count is taken by the keepers, who inspect each cell. This generally occupies about half an hour; afterwards, the men are released to wash up before the morning meal.

Breakfast is served in the mess hall one hour after the rising bell. The meal usually consists of prison hash, a cereal, and coffee. At ten minutes of eight, a whistle is blown and the men report to their shops or their companies, if they are working in the yard. Another count is taken, and promptly at eight o'clock, the daily work is begun. Each prisoner has his own work to do, and there must be no lagging. While old methods of discipline have been done away with, modern methods are not lenient and the men must keep busy turning out the amount of work assigned to them.

Work continues steadily from eight until twelve, when the whistle blows for the noonday meal. Under the charge of Mutual Welfare League officers, the men are formed into companies and marched into the mess hall for dinner, consisting of some wholesome but coarse meat and vegetable. The appropriation for prison food is exceedingly small; in fact, it is the same as of sixty years ago, so only the plainest of food can be served.

FIGURE 7. The mess hall at Sing Sing c. 1890. The food served at the prison greatly improved from 1879 to 1929. Photo courtesy of the Ossining Historical Society.

After dinner, the men are allowed a brief respite until 12:50 P.M., when the whistle blows again and summons them to work. The count is repeated and work continues until 4 P.M., when a light supper, usually some cold meat or fruit, is served in the mess hall. Some of the men prefer to prepare their own meal at this time. They are allowed to purchase food from the prison store and, in this way, find a change from the monotony of prison fare.

After supper, the men are allowed to walk about, smoke, play ball, or just talk until 8:30 P.M., when the whistle blows calling them to their cells. Another count is taken and the men are locked in for the night. On Tuesdays and Fridays, they are allowed a short time during the evening to attend the movies which are shown under the auspices of the Mutual Welfare League. These motion pictures are very much enjoyed and help in keeping up morale.

FIGURE 8. The new chapel c. 1929, where services were held for Catholics, Protestants, Jews, and Christian Scientists. Various forms of entertainment were also presented here. Photo courtesy of the Ossining Historical Society.

Chapel services are held every Sunday morning at nine o'clock. Attendance is not compulsory, but the men who do not attend must remain in their cells until after the services. These services include Catholic, Protestant, Hebrew, and Christian Science. The attendance is most encouraging. The new chapel building is a magnificent structure so planned that it may be partitioned off for the various services. When the huge sliding doors are thrown open, there is seating capacity for the entire personnel of the institution, and many forms of entertainment are enjoyed at frequent intervals. There are four chaplains in the institution—Rev. John P. McCaffrey, Catholic; Rev. Anthony Peterson, Protestant; Rev. Jacob Katz, Jewish; and Rev. John Tillotson, Christian Science. Father McCaffrey recently succeeded Father Cashin when the latter was transferred to the Tombs prison in New York City. He supervises the entire religious activity at Sing

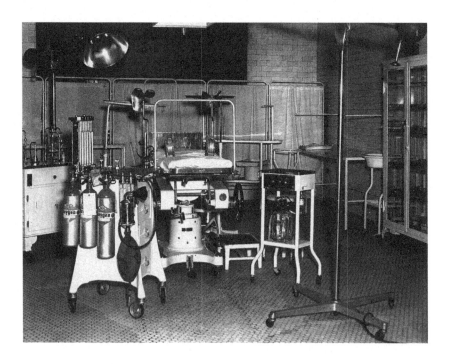

FIGURE 9. The Sing Sing Prison hospital c. 1929 was well equipped for inmate medical exams and surgeries. Photo courtesy of Guy Cheli.

Sing; though, of course, each chaplain retains complete jurisdiction over his own particular creed.

The hospital is one of the best equipped buildings in the institution. On the first floor, there is a modern X-ray apparatus and its various accessories, three rooms for the physician in charge of the venereal examinations, a surgical laboratory, rooms fitted for the examination of the eyes, ears, and throat, a psychiatric and psychological examining room, a dental operating room, and a laboratory for staff working in the diagnostic and examination rooms.

The second floor consists of a museum, a records room, a library, and a lecture room. On the third floor there are separate surgical wards for major and minor operations. The acute and chronic cases are kept separate from one another. The fourth or top floor contains a complete operating unit with two operating rooms—one for major and one for minor operations. Each has separate sterilization facilities together with preparation, etherizing, and recovery rooms. The rest of the floor is given up to a convalescent solarium and quarters for the male nurses.

The hospital is used for detailed observation and treatment and as a school for the education of medical attendants. Skilled nursing care in prisons is in direct proportion to the nurses' medical knowledge as it directly relates to the particular health problems of a prison community.

Sing Sing, as it is today, is a model penal institution. Now, let us go back to the beginnings of Sing Sing and trace its development from a "place of the living dead" to the current institution, which some people now choose to regard as a "hotel."

~

During the years 1820 to 1824, it became apparent that New York City and the eastern part of the state needed a new prison. The original prison was situated near what is now the slip of the Christopher Street ferry. It was called Newgate Prison and its erection was begun in 1796. By 1820, the city had outgrown this structure and it was found to be improperly constructed.

> A commission was appointed to find a suitable site for the new building. They considered Governor's Island and several other islands in the harbor at New York in addition to a site just across the river atop the Palisades. Marble Hill, just across the Spuyten Duyvil Creek at the northern tip of Manhattan, was also considered, but none of those places proved to be what was desired.
>
> Finally, while on a trip up the Hudson River, the commissioners were attracted by a fine, wooded knoll rising nearly two hundred feet above the eastern bank. The land was the property of a farmer, John Fleetwood Marsh, and he had named the territory Mount Pleasant.

The hill, which was of stone, offered two things—material out of which to build the new prison and work for the inmates after completion of the structure. The convicts would be able to quarry marble out of the hillside for building purposes in the cities of the East.

The commission approved this site and the State purchased the land—some hundred and thirty acres—from Mr. Marsh. A decision was reached to build the prison as near the water's edge as possible so that everything would be accessible to the river. This land was nothing but a swamp and had to be filled in with debris from the quarry.

The prison was first called Mount Pleasant Prison; that name appears in official documents. Gradually, it became known—at length officially—by the arresting name of the nearby village, Sing Sing. Then, in turnabout fashion, the village grew to be self-conscious after a time and renamed itself Ossining.[2]

The name Sing Sing was derived from a tribe of Indians known as the Sint Sincks who inhabited this locality many years ago and referred to it as Sink Sink, meaning stone upon stone. The villagers had considerable trouble in changing the name of their community, but finally succeeded in 1901 to have the village name changed to Ossining. The following is a recount of the initial building of Sing Sing:

On the 15th of May, 1825, a fleet of scows was towed down the Hudson River and made fast to the banks where Sing Sing Prison now casts its menacing shadow of gloom. On board of the scows was a motley crew of one hundred manacled convicts, under command of Captain Elam Lynde, transported from Auburn to construct a new prison to relieve the congested conditions . . .

Quarries were quickly opened up by the convicts and blocks of white sandstone were dragged from the hillside and piled one on another until the great Cell Block of today where countless thousands of human derelicts have ever since been confined, was ready for occupancy. Imagine the thoughts of the men who built it when they found themselves locked in the narrow stone holes, no bigger than a dead man's grave, that are designated as cells! There were twelve hundred of these cells. A dog might rebel at being forced to use one for a kennel. Yet more than fifty thousand aching hearts have been locked in them during over a century that has elapsed since the dank and smelly quarters were first opened for habitation.

It was a grim joker who christened the new bastile, Mount Pleasant Prison. A more appropriate name would have been the Cemetery of Dead Hopes. The name provoked so much mirth and ridicule that it was later changed to Sing Sing which, in Chinese, means Hail! Hail! They soon had the gang all here for hundreds of new prisoners were brought up from New York to swell the ranks of the original one hundred who came from Auburn.

Captain Lynd, whose cruel and merciless architecture remains a monument to his memory, was appointed warden. He has long been dead, God rest his soul! Many came after him, but none were more execrated.

He chained his prisoners together and kept them at work in the quarries until they dug out of the earth stone to build the State Capitol of Albany . . .[3]

The old Cell Block remains today exactly as it was when constructed by convict labor in 1825. The walls, floor, and ceiling are entirely of stone. The dimensions of each cell are: seven feet long, three feet three inches wide, and six feet seven inches high. The doors, twenty-two inches wide, are of plate steel with a checkerboard latticework comprising the upper half and are double locked.

The tiers of the cells, rising six high, are set back to back and the front of the tiers, reached by narrow galleries, is about ten feet from the enclosing walls of the big building . . . Each cell contains an iron cot with straw or

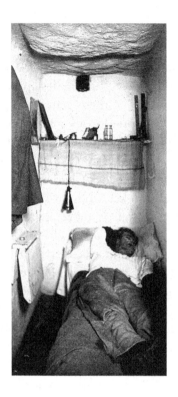

FIGURE 10. The cells in the old cell block were only 3 feet 3 inches wide and made entirely of stone. Photo courtesy of Guy Cheli.

Tampico mattress, pillow and blankets, electric light, a tin drinking cup and the prisoner's iron slop bucket."[4]

Improvements have been made in the form of larger windows for better air and sunlight, radio earphones at the head of each bed, and various devices for overcoming floor moisture. There is no modern plumbing, however, and the bucket is still used in this building. Since the completion of the new cell block, the old one has been used almost exclusively for the reception of new prisoners.

The cells of the new cell block are four feet wide, seven feet six inches long and seven feet high. Each has a large window which

Cell· New Prison

FIGURE 11. Cells in the new cell block are larger and equipped with a toilet instead of a bucket. Photo courtesy of Guy Cheli.

admits plenty of air and sunlight. The furnishings include a single bed, a mirror, a desk, a chair, a basin with hot and cold running water and a toilet. There is no latticework on the cell door. It is open all the way down to the floor and the bars are set about three inches apart.

In spite of the uncomfortable surroundings in the old cell block, many of the men were optimistic and the following is an instance:

A man who came here and spent a night of sleepless horror his first night in the Cell Block set about the next day trying to improve what must be endured . . . The only ventilation was through the small openings of the latticed upper half of the cell door, but he was lucky enough to have been assigned to a cell that was opposite a large window. He found when this window was open that enough fresh air entered his cell to fill his lungs.

There was a hard, narrow bunk made fast to the wall. It was the only furnishing save that, on the bunk, was a tick filled with musty excelsior and a pair of blankets mostly of cotton. The floor, walls, and ceiling were rough sandstone, every crevice alive with bugs. The attempt to sleep was torment. The next day, he obtained permission to scrub his cell with hot soapsuds and to spray it with a chemical that would kill the pests that had kept him awake. To complete the job, he smoked them out with a smudge and he found some cement to stop up the crevices that had been used for breeding purposes.

He had a talk with the Principal Keeper and found that the regulations would permit him to do the very things he most wished to do for his comfort. With the funds he had deposited to his credit when he entered prison, by denying himself cigarettes and some similar luxuries, he was enabled to purchase from a shop in the village, a small, enameled, white cot with woven wire springs, a comfortable mattress, good quality blankets, pillows and two changes of bed linen. For his floor, he obtained from the same shop a rag rug of attractive colors. The entire outlay was less than fifty dollars.

Another prisoner, about to be discharged, presented him with a small cabinet with lock and key for his belongings and a prison-made writing table that folded against the wall when not in use. Some scraps of wire were bent into shape for hooks and inserted into the stone walls to hang things on. An inmate carpenter fashioned boards to make three shelves, and another inmate decorated them with drawn-work covers. The prisoner found some pieces of broken glass that had gone into scrap and cut them into shape. With strips of colored paper, they became frames for photographs and pictures cut from magazines. Pegs were inserted into the walls to hang them on.

In less than a week, a dingy hole which so closely resembled a newly dug grave was converted into what appears, and really is, a comparatively comfortable sleeping nest. Many a man aboard a yacht has slept in a cabin as small and stuffier and imagined that he was having the time of his life. It all depends upon the state of mind. One can make almost any place in which Fate has cast him a hell or paradise.[5]

The above was written by an inmate and shows quite clearly the manner in which some accepted their fate and made themselves as comfortable as possible under the circumstances.

The old cell block has seen many strange characters. Men of great notoriety gained through crime served terms in Sing Sing during the early years of its establishment. Today, we have the holdup man, the gangster, the racketeer and others, but these terms are merely creations in the language of the day. They are lurid terms at best. We did not know their use—never heard of them—a few years ago. The average criminal of today is charged with the commission of crimes which were unheard of years ago. If the ghosts of the criminals—those men of the criminal world who have passed on—were to be paraded through the prison yard today, what a vastly different galaxy they would represent! We would see Charles E. Beckwith, who robbed B. T. Babbitt, millionaire soap manufacturer, by falsifying his records; Captain Trelaw, né Cornelius Alvord, Jr., who stole almost $700,000 from the First National Bank by making false entries in the books; Monroe Edwards, who, after being sentenced for forgery, forged President Andrew Jackson's signature to a pardon for himself, failing, however, to be released; Quimbo Appo, a Chinaman who killed his white wife in New York and was, for years, the only man of his race in an American penitentiary; Roland B. Molineux, who spent years in the death house and later wrote a book of his experiences called "The House With the Little Green Door"; John J.

Scannell, companion of Richard Croker while the latter was boss of Tammany Hall in 1898; John Y. McKane, the Czar of Coney Island, whose famous injunctions caused him to be sentenced for six years by Judge Gaynor, later mayor of New York City; and many others. If all these notorious criminals were to be contrasted with those of today, what a radical difference would be noticed! These old-timers were middle-aged men while the vast majority of the present inmates are in their early twenties.

Many more attained notoriety by breaking out of the old prison. These men are best remembered by keepers and convicts alike. There were many more escapes back then than now. Necessity is the mother of invention, and the methods employed by inmates seeking freedom are both uncanny and ingenious. The tale of the "Duck Prison Breaker" will doubtless always remain one of the most brilliant and daring escapes ever attempted at Sing Sing.

James Dunn, alias Foster, came to Sing Sing by way of the Tombs in 1864. He had been sentenced to ten years imprisonment for burglary. After a time, he grew bored with his new surrounds and decided he wanted to be free. While waiting for an opportunity to escape, he noticed that there were numerous wild ducks on and about the river where the walls of Sing Sing run down to the water's edge. It had once been permissible to shoot these birds, but an earlier prison warden had issued orders against the practice on the ground that the reports of the weapons put the prison on alert and brought out the guards.

Dunn was aware of this order and decided to swim a "duck" to freedom somewhat in the manner of Sinbad escaping from the Valley of Diamonds. Being something of a wood carver, Dunn fashioned a realistic duck decoy from a block of wood. He managed to paint the duck decoy, a smear at a time, in the print shop. Next, he feigned illness in order to be confined to the hospital for a few days. While there, he managed to appropriate a piece of rubber tubing and a square sheet of the same material. With the aid of a little cloth, thread, and glue, he made a mask. He ran one end of the tube through the mask in such a manner that it would fit into his mouth, thus providing a means of securing air while he would be under water.

Dunn's opportunity was not long in coming for he was soon put to work on the marble loading docks. He worked steadily for several days so that he might ascertain the actions and habits of his guards before he made his escape. He managed to slip by the roving eyes of the guards for a few moments—just long enough to enable him to prepare for his submarine adventure. He tied the free end of the tubing to the mask, put a few stones in his pocket to hold himself under the water, and waded out into the Hudson. Submerged, he half swam, half walked about a mile downstream. Crawling out upon the bank, he wrung out his clothes and hid until confederates arrived with money and a change of apparel.

His escape was a success, but about a year later, he was returned to prison for another burglary. After some delay, he tried his trick again, fooling himself into believing that the officers had not heard of his prior escape. His overconfidence did not pan out this time for a keeper took the duck away, telling him to carve parrots if he must devote his talents to ornithology in wood.

Prisoners would stop at nothing to break out of prison. Knowing the conditions as they were, one can hardly blame the men. They were all gamblers at heart with the idea that they had everything to gain and nothing to lose. A man thinks very little about his freedom until it is taken away from him. Then, he will do everything possible to regain it regardless of the consequences. An instance similar to the "Duck Prison Break" occurred during the first years of my service at Sing Sing. This fellow must have been an understudy to Dunn because he used practically the same method.

The prisoner, whose name I have forgotten, made himself a rough diver's suit in the tailor shop and hid it in a pile of rubbish near the docks. When the chance came, he waded out into the river, launched his wood duck with the rubber tubing attached and walked northward along the bottom for about a mile to Brandreth's Pill Factory. There, the man came out on the bank, pressed the water from his underwear after discarding the striped suit and managed to attract the attention of some of the workers in the factory. He implored them to give him shelter and clothing. Doctor Brandreth was called. The convict told the doctor that he had been swimming while someone had stolen his clothes as a practical joke. It never occurred to the kindly pellet-maker that this might be a desperate criminal from the institution so nearby. He supplied the man with a suit of clothes, a bit of money and sent him on his way, rejoicing. It was not until hours after that the good doctor became aware of his charitable mistake.

~

At the time of my entrance on November 1, 1879, Sing Sing Prison was in its fifty-fourth year. Since its establishment, the number of

FIGURE 12. Prisoners worked in silence and were required to complete a certain amount of work or be punished. Photo courtesy of the Ossining Historical Society.

inmates housed there has grown rapidly. The total number of men confined was at 2,300 as compared with 1,800 at Clinton. Sing Sing's buildings were more modern and the men were handled in a more efficient manner, but the life of the inmates was practically the same. Disciplinary measures had been stern at Clinton. They were even more so at Sing Sing.

I was ushered into the office of Warden Brush within a few moments after the massive iron gates had clanged shut behind me. This time, however, I was prepared and experienced no qualms at the sound. The guard who had admitted me led the way through the busy prison yard to the office. The atmosphere of the place was significantly different from that at Clinton. The keepers were much younger and snappier. Everyone was bustling about. I could see at a glance that laziness or indifference was not tolerated. I realized the warden of such an institution must be a very capable man.

As I entered his office, my attention was attracted to an inscription in the floor just over the threshold, "Errare humanum est" (To err is human). This phrase struck me as peculiar, especially so in the office of the prison head. However, Warden Brush had risen to greet me, and I dismissed the thought from my mind.

"Welcome to Sing Sing, Mr. Conyes," said the warden. "According to this letter from Mr. Fuller, you are one of the finest attendants he ever had in his employ. He even goes so far as to recommend you as a keeper from the start. Well, I'm afraid I can't let you have that position so soon. It is customary at this institution to break the new men in as guards until they prove their ability. No doubt you are all this letter implies, but after all, a rule is a rule, you know. We have some mighty tough characters here. You'll have to show me that you can handle them before I take the chance of allowing you such authority."

This news was not good. The difference of ten dollars a month in pay was considerable to a man of my means. I argued with the warden, trying to make him see things from my viewpoint, but there had never been any exceptions to this rule at Sing Sing. I told him how Warden Fuller had made me a keeper from the first day.

"That doesn't mean a thing here," replied the warden. "You can either take a guard's pay or give up any desire you may have of working here. Let's not beat around the bush any longer. Are you going to take what we have or not?"

His last comment left me with no alternatives, so I said, "Well, Warden, if that's your rule I'll abide by it, but let me tell you that I don't care for the idea."

The warden smiled and assigned me to duty patrolling the wall of the prison. This work was of an entirely different nature from what I had formerly done. Regardless of my feelings, I threw myself into the new task determined to show Mr. Brush my qualifications merited a keeper position.

Parading up and down along the top of that wall in all kinds of weather was no easy task. After a time, it became terribly monotonous, but the warden showed no sign of transferring me. Finally, I went to him and told him that unless he made me a keeper at once, I was going to resign.

"Now listen, Mr. Conyes, you came here with the best of recommendations. I warn you that if you try to resign, I shall refuse to accept your resignation. I understand how you feel about this thing. Go back on the wall for one more week. At the end of that time, I'll see what I can do for you."

Before the end of the week, however, the Civil Service Law went into effect. All employees in the civil service had to prove their ability to do their particular work by taking the prescribed tests. I obtained a leave of absence and left for Albany to take the examination for a prison official. My past experience proved helpful and the result was most gratifying. All doubt was removed. I had become eligible for a keeper's post, and I meant to get it. Upon my return to the prison, Warden Brush was the first to offer his congratulations and assigned me to keeper duty at once in the emory room of the stove shop. Now, at least, I would be off the prison wall and my surroundings would be a bit more pleasant.

In the emory room, prisoners cut patterns out of the raw material and even up the rough metal edges. Then, the pieces were sent to the assembling room. The contract for this work was with the Perry Stove Company. In addition to myself, there was an instructor who helped the men learn the trade and saw that the work was done

FIGURE 13. In the emory room, prisoners worked for pennies under contract making stoves for the Perry Stove Company. Photo courtesy of the Albany Institute of History and Art.

properly. My duty was to keep the men—all fifty of them—in order. I had little to do with the work itself, since I knew nothing about it.

Working in the emory room was quite difficult. The dust and fine metal particles, created by the spinning of the emory wheels, filled the room at all times. Only the strongest and most hardened men could stand such an atmosphere. This resulted in having some of the worst characters in the institution under my jurisdiction. The emory room had a reputation for numerous fights and riots among its workers. Consequently, keepers and men were changed off every eight months.

FIGURE 14. Alfred Conyes's billy clubs. Photo from the Conyes family archives.

Shortly after I took charge of this place, the men tried to get the upper hand through sheer viciousness. I was none too sure of myself, but when it became necessary, I waded in, knocked a few around and generally made them understand that regardless of their past actions, they were to behave themselves as long as I had something to say about it. After that first week, the men settled down and offered no trouble for almost ten months. This conduct was just too good to last. I had a few suspicions as to what might be formulating beneath the comparatively quiet exterior of the men.

The instructor had witnessed riots in the emory room and congratulated me upon the attitude which, to all appearances, I had instilled within the men. It was then that the anticipated trouble began.

While the instructor was talking, I happened to glance up because of a commotion at the far end of the room. I saw two men struggling. Rushing over, I noticed that one of them, a Negro, had fastened his teeth into an ear of the other. He had been getting the worst of the fight and decided that this was the only way to gain the upper hand. Taking out my stout hickory club which is carried by all keepers for just such emergencies, I tapped the Negro on the shoulder: "Let go of that ear, big boy, or I'll have to bounce this over your skull," I shouted, brandishing the club. He rolled his eyes, shook his head, and bit harder.

Since the man had disregarded all my persuading, I struck him on the head with my club and he sank to the floor. He came to a few moments later, opened his eyes, and smiled up at me. Opening his mouth, he showed me the ear which he had bitten off. Before I realized what he was doing, he had swallowed it.

"If yo' hadn't jumped on, Mistah Conyes, Ah woulda' eaten 'im alive," he grinned as he pointed to his adversary.

I had seen gruesome things in prison, but this was something new for me. I had thought cannibalism was extinct in the United

FIGURE 15. Doing as he was told, Alfred Conyes put prisoners into the solitary confinement cells as part of their punishment determined by the principal keeper. Photo courtesy of Guy Cheli.

States. I reported the Negro to the principal keeper, who sentenced him to solitary confinement on bread and water. First, however, my order was to "hang him up" for a while. Keepers and guards have always been pictured as the bullying type. This is purely the product of some imaginative minds. A duty has to be done no matter how distasteful it may be to the parties concerned. In spite of what the man had done, I didn't care to see him "hung up." Still, the punishment was one which he might remember, so I did as I was told. Later, when he was released from the dungeon, the Negro became one of the most obedient men under me.

Convicts would invariably take advantage of any little kindnesses extended to them. I had to be most discriminating in matters of this sort. I allowed certain privileges, but believe me, the men had to work to get them. Then, too, privileges were easily lost. If a man worked well without continually growling, I would see that he received the best of treatment, harsh as it may have seemed to an outsider. Of course, there were many who were stubborn and simply wouldn't work for any reason. I had to "ride" these and resort to force when necessary.

The working details were formed in companies, each under the charge of a keeper. The best men, known as leaders, were placed on the ends of each rank. When we were to march into the mess hall, I would line them up in two ranks and take the count to check up on the absentees. Then a command would be given to face in one direction or another and they would march off.

There had been considerable talking in my company during these marches to mess. I had overlooked it once in a while because it helped keep up the morale of the men. As in other cases, they took advantage of this until they had overdone the privilege, so I told them there would be no more talking. One of the men paid no attention. His constant babbling got on my nerves. I had warned him, time after time, but he persisted in keeping his mouth wagging. There was nothing left to do, but report him to the P. K. My orders were to treat him the same as the Negro. After he had been in the dungeon for a while, the inmate sent for me and promised to behave in the future. Perhaps he thought I would ask the P. K. to have him released before his time was up. However, I did no such thing and he spent the allotted time there before coming back to work. His attitude was much better, and he kept his mouth shut when told to from that time on.

These two incidents were the only disruptions to a quiet year in the emory room. The prescribed period of eight months service in this shop had long since passed. Long hours in the emory room were beginning to take a toll on me. I wondered why the P. K. had not seen fit to transfer me to some other post. Knowing he had many things on his mind, I did not want to bother him about such a small matter. Finally, I spoke to another keeper about the length of time I had been at this same post. He was surprised to hear of it and said I should ask the warden for a transfer at once. I said nothing more, but decided to wait for a short time before I went in to see him.

I was saved the trouble, however, for the P. K. sent for me and asked me how long I had been in the emory room. Knowing my friend must have spoken for me, I replied that I had been there for seventeen months.

FIGURE 16. After working in the emory room of the stove shop, Conyes was assigned to the laundry. Photo courtesy of the Ossining Historical Society.

"Well, well, Mr. Conyes, time certainly does fly by," said the P. K. "I had no idea that you had been in there that long. I'm sorry this hasn't been brought to my attention before. You should have spoken to me about it. Certainly, I shall transfer you. You've done mighty well since you have been with us. I think you'll find the starch room of the laundry suitable. I'll have the present keeper there transferred to your old place. Here, I'll give you a note and you can tell him yourself."

Thanking the P. K., I went to the laundry to notify the keeper there of his hard luck. He seemed pleased with the news for a reason which I was to discover later. The only thought in my mind was elation at finally leaving the emory room.

In the laundry, we handled shirts for a firm in New York City. They sent their shirts up the river to Sing Sing, where they were washed, starched, dried, and ironed by the convicts. Then, after being placed in huge packing cases, they were sent back to the city.

The work of drying and starching the shirts was carried out by the men in my company. This room was situated in an old wooden building, and extra precautions had to be taken against fire. There were fifty men here—the same number as in the emory room. By this time, I was well aware of the "tricks of the trade" and had little trouble keeping a close watch on every man.

The entire atmosphere of the laundry was ever so much better than that of the old emory room. I was quite pleased with my new post. The men worked well and offered little resistance to my commands. However, several incidents occurred which are worthy of mention.

David Murray had always been a faithful worker. The keepers liked him, and he had never caused any trouble up until when he tried to make his escape. With the help of some friends, he had himself nailed up in a packing case like those in which the shirts were shipped. He took tools with him so he could cut his way out once the prison had been left behind. Everything went well until the crates were loaded onto the truck. Murray's associates became mixed-up and set his crate on the truck upside down, leaving Murray standing on his head. The truck drove off giving Murray the worst ride of his life over the bumpiest of roads. It was a wonder to me how the man ever lived through it. When the driver stopped to unload the crates to the station platform, he was surprised to hear a faint tapping from within one of the boxes. He investigated. Murray tumbled out half dead from the jolting he had received while standing on his head. He told me later that it was impossible for him to go on after that ride. Once again within the prison walls, he spent fifteen days in the dungeon and thought better of trying to escape again.

Then, on February 13, 1883, a sensational riot broke out in the prison. Two hundred prisoners employed in the laundry area had found fault with their work and called a strike. A great deal of property of the laundry contractors, Perry and Co., stove contractors, and other concerns employing prison labor was wrecked. During the outbreak, a Negro smashed approximately $10,000 worth of stove patterns in the stove shop, holding up the work for over three days. The health of P. K. Jesse Dixon broke down and Warden Brush had to excuse him from further duty in quelling the strikers.

Assemblyman Keyes, on the prisoners' behalf, introduced a bill to abolish contract labor in prisons. In the years to come, the contract system was ended along with the overworking of prisoners for the contractors' profits.

Shortly after this strike, I had occasion to lock up a young fellow who was still in his knee breeches. We only get prisoners who are sixteen or older now, but this one was far below that age. The lad had been sent to the reformatory. While there, he had a quarrel with another boy and cut him with a knife. As punishment, he was sentenced to Sing Sing for seven years. Just a kid—that's all he was.

Come along Christmas time, I looked in his cell. Up to then, the kid had been game enough, but now he was crying—crying just like any other youngster.

"What's the matter, kid?" I asked.

"Well, sir, this is Christmas Eve. I used to hang up my stocking for Santa Claus to come when I was home. He came every time too. Guess I just can't help cryin' 'cause I haven't been very good this year and I'm afraid he won't be able to get into this place even if he wants to."

The boy was in Sing Sing, but he was only a kid after all, so I said: "Boy, you go ahead and hang up that stocking. Here's a piece of string. You can fasten it around the bars somehow. Then, we'll see what happens. This place isn't a very nice one for Santa Claus to come to, but you never can tell about him. I'm not saying he will be able to get through these stone walls—they are pretty solid and we have no chimney, but he may be able to get through somehow."

A little later, as I passed the boy's cell on my way off duty, I noticed the stocking hanging from his door. The night relief was just coming on, and I asked them to do what they could for the little fellow carefully explaining my conversation with him.

We all watched when he awoke the next morning. His eyes bulged right out. There was his stocking—crammed full of apples, oranges, nuts, and candy. The kid was so happy he couldn't talk. Finding that stocking so full did him a lot of good.

A short time after, he was allowed to go home. I spoke to him as he was leaving: "Now, boy you had better keep out of here because Santa Claus may not be able to get in at all the next time."

"Don't worry, Mr. Conyes," said the little fellow. "You'll never see me again in a place like this. I've had enough. I'm goin' home to my mother and stay there. Good-bye."

I watched him as he started down the road—just a little fellow; almost running he was so happy. I sighed and turned back toward the grim, gray cell block. Free! What a wonderful feeling that youngster must have had when he found himself on the outside looking in.

Work continued right along in my shop, and the warden expressed to me that he was pleased with the results I had obtained. The shirt contract was steadily growing because the firm which had the contract considered our work of the highest order. We had not lost a single shirt until the day when a fire broke out in the drying kiln.

We had our hands full because the flames threatened to ignite the wooden structure at any moment. I ordered the men to fill their wash-kits with water to throw on the flames. Now, if ever there was an opportunity for escape, this was it, but they didn't take advantage of it. Instead, all plunged in working like mad until we finally had the fire under control. Several of the men sustained severe burns, but not one made a break for freedom in the confusion. They might have caused me no end of trouble, but they chose the better way, for which I was more than thankful.

Beyond these instances, there were no more disturbances in the laundry. Many of the men called me by name, while I was, at all times, glad to meet them halfway. This was contrary to regulations, but I found that I could get more work out of them if I treated them well. This idea was not so well thought of in these days, but it has proved most successful in modern penal institutions.

Shortly after the fire, the principal keeper called me into his office. Wondering what was coming next, I sat down.

"How are you getting along, Conyes?"

"Very well, sir," I replied, thinking this was the appropriate answer.

"The foreman of the shoe shop," said the P. K., "has asked me to transfer you to his place. Says he comes from some place up near your hometown. You'll be a keeper there, of course. I told him I would see how you felt about it."

"Why certainly," I replied. "I have been in the laundry quite awhile. I would like the change if it is all right with you, P. K."

"That's settled then, Conyes. I'll have someone relieve you in the laundry. Better wait until tomorrow before you change. That's all."

My relief came around promptly the next day. I went over to the shoe shop. Sure enough, the instructor knew a great deal about the section of Ulster County from where I came. This post seemed to be the best yet. We had a great deal in common and spent many pleasant hours working together. My newly found friend was a pleasant companion.

Lost Souls Sewing on Soles

In the shoe shop, each inmate has a separate and distinct job whether it is cutting out patterns or sewing on the soles. A fixed amount of work has to be accomplished every day by each man. My main duty, in addition to preserving order in the shop, was to see that the specified amount of shoes were turned out daily. The instructor was a most capable fellow and had succeeded in developing some very skillful shoemakers out of the detail. Very few of the men knew what shoemaking was all about at the start, but by patience and kindness, my friend had accomplished teaching them the trade.

All of the men were good fellows and their attitude was the most genial of any in the prison. They did as they were told and I never heard any grumbling about my methods until a few new men came in from another shop. I had to punish two of these for open insubordination. The general behavior had been so good; I did not intend to let them ruin it.

A certain time, designated as "hospital call," was set aside each morning during which those who felt the need of medical attention were allowed to go to the hospital and have their wants attended. After that time, however, no one could go unless they had been injured in some way during the day.

One morning, long after "hospital call," the two men came to me and requested permission to see the doctor. "Men," I replied, "you know as well as everyone else that the time for this sort of thing was up long ago. Why ask me about it? I can't let you go and you know it. Don't argue because you'll be wasting your breath. Now, get back to work." They grumbled for a moment or so, but went back to their work. They were both "leaders" in the company. When I lined the men up after working hours and gave the command to move off, the first refused to move. I told him to fall out and repeated the command. The next also refused to budge so I had him fall out beside the other. At the third command, the men marched off and I had no further trouble. Then I turned to the two men and asked their reason for refusing to obey my order. They replied that they had made up their minds not to work for me since I had not allowed them to go to the hospital earlier in the day. I called the rules to their attention once again and reported them to Principal Keeper Connaughton. Next day, I took these two fellows out, "hung them up," and threw them into separate dungeons where they remained for fifteen days. At the end of this time, they again reported for work. When we lined up for mess, these two men fell into their usual place as "leaders."

"Listen here, men," I said, "you no longer deserve your old positions. You have shown me quite clearly that you are not to be trusted. Now, get back in the rear rank and stay there where you belong. You might as well know here and now that disobeying my orders will only land you in 'solitary.'" After a few weeks, when I thought they had had enough, I allowed them to take up their old positions. They never troubled me again and became my most dependable assistants.

The very next day, I found one of the men, a Negro, making a "crooked" shoe. Anything "crooked" in prison labor is work done under cover in addition to the required labor. Inmates often tried to make things for themselves in this way. I went over to this darky, took the shoe away, and asked him why he was making an extra one.

"Well, Mistah Conyes," he replied, "it's this way. Ah'm makin' dat dere shoe foah a one legged man. Dat's what Ah'm doin'." Since he had always been one of my best men, I let the Negro off with a warning not to let it happen again.

At about this time, Johnny Hope was admitted to Sing Sing. One of the most notorious criminals of his day, he had tunneled for a year and a half under the Manhattan Bank in New York City. Finally, in 1878, he managed to get inside the vault and cleaned it out of a million dollars in cash.

I was on Hope's reception committee when he arrived at the prison to serve a twenty-year term. The man was completely broken and tears streamed rapidly down his face. Later, he took a grip on himself and proved to be one of the best characters in the institution. Indeed, he wasn't a bad chap at all.

~

When I was still in the shoe shop, one New Year's Eve, there was plenty of excitement in and about the prison. Word had reached Warden Brush that "Red" Leary and his fearless gang of bank robbers, who were credited with the great Northampton, Massachusetts, bank robbery in 1876, were on their way to Sing Sing to raid the prison and deliver from prison the imprisoned members of the safe-blowing fraternity.

I was one of the prison force summoned to do extra duty that night. A cordon of guards, armed with repeating rifles, was thrown around the prison premises. Heavily armed posses under Police Chief McNeal were watching the Sing Sing depot and the bank further up the street.

The all-night vigil proved unwarranted for Leary's gang never appeared. A mysterious delegation had arrived in town by boat. They were taken for cracksmen, but later proved to be a Yonkers hotel keeper and some other horsemen who came to the village to buy horses. The fuss which the authorities made in their preparations for Leary may seem somewhat extreme judging by the result, but we could not afford to ignore any warnings of that sort. It was too dangerous and the old type of criminal might be expected to commit all kinds of violence.

Since the construction of the prison buildings in 1825, the quarries at Sing Sing had been deserted. The finest kind of stone

Figure 17. Quarrying and cutting stone was difficult work that required skill and precision. Photo courtesy of the Ossining Historical Society.

was right on the prison property within the walls for the taking. The state finally decided to use these quarries for additional revenue. Money was badly needed, and the stone offered a means to secure it. Accordingly, contracts were let out for cemetery monuments. Warden Brush had sent out a questionnaire in which vocations before prison work was the topic stressed. After looking over the answers, he called me into his office and informed me that I was the only official in the institution who had previously worked in stone. When asked if I knew enough about the trade to take up a position as keeper and instructor in the quarries, I replied that I felt quite capable of discharging those duties in a satisfactory manner. The job was mine and I started in at once in the stone shed, the warden having decided that it was the best place for me. Now, I was right in my element. I never would have thought I would be cutting stone in prison when, a short time back, I had been doing the same thing on my father's farm.

Some of the prisoners had previously worked in quarries. Believe me, I was not long in recognizing these few from the others, however few they were. These men I designated as my assistants. We had our hands full instructing the new recruits in the intricacies of a sledge and maul. Anyone can use these instruments in a more or less awkward way, but it takes constant practice to handle them so that the stone will not be haggled and broken to bits in a slovenly manner. I knew from my earlier apprenticeship that there is an art to stonecutting.

Working in stone under a roof had its disadvantages. The Perry Stove contract had run out a short time before and the old foundry became the new stone shed. The fine particles of dust got into our eyes and, if we worked there long enough, into our lungs. Such labor should always be done in the outside air, but here at Sing Sing the shed was the only available space. In spite of the many difficulties, however, we managed quite well.

Once the stone was quarried, it was brought into the shed, where we cut, shaped, and smoothed over the huge slabs. Afterwards, we did all the necessary polishing and lettering. Upon completion of the work, the monuments were shipped out to the contractor to be sold as he saw fit.

My company numbered one hundred and thirty men. Believe me, they were tough. When I first looked them over, I thought the warden had dumped his very worst men on me. The majority of the men were thoroughly bad, and I was constantly "on my toes." In a way, though, I was glad to have them so tough because the work was extremely difficult—more difficult than anything has been since. There were one or two who could not stand the physical strain, but the larger part of the men stood it very well—surprisingly so, in view of the prison meals at the time.

It was during my time in this shop that my most interesting experiences took place. There was always plenty of excitement, and no prison officials seemed anxious to take my place. I felt confident in my abilities, however. I knew the work and thought I could handle the men under any and all conditions.

One day, when the signal came for the men to go to work, they refused. I questioned them as to their motive. They replied that they were not getting sufficient food to enable them to do such hard labor. Inwardly, I agreed with them, but I could not allow myself to be interested in what they had to eat. That was their lookout. My job was to put them to work and keep them working. I could see by their attitude that I was in for plenty of trouble and scarcely knew what to do for a moment. Anyone would feel uncomfortable standing before a hundred and thirty men who, armed with picks and sledges, dared you to make them go to work. I gave them five minutes to think things over before I rang the bell again. If they refused, I told the men, I would come after them and make them work. The five minutes was given more to allow me to recover my composure than to let the men think. I doubted if many had anything to rethink. My pretty speech had been more bravado than anything, but I could not let them know I was rapidly becoming rattled.

When time was up, I rang the bell. Half of the men began to work. The rest refused, and with picks and sledges pounced upon those who were working in an effort to disable them. This would never do, so I had to step in with my hickory club. It was a hot time for a few moments. When it was over, some of the men went to the hospital while others nursed broken noses, cut lips and broken bones. The uninjured went back to work, and after the debris had been cleared away, the stone shed became calm once more.

Later in the week, I saw the stone contractor and suggested he pay the men extra for any overtime work which they managed to do. He agreed with my proposal. The men turned in and worked doubly hard now that they could earn more for their extra work. Some of them earned as much as seventy-five cents and a dollar a day. This money was used to buy food which they all shared alike. They thanked me too—not only for the food, but for keeping them from killing each other during the fight. They all thought I had prevented them from going to the chair.

A short time after, another of the men refused to work. I had repeatedly warned him for falling behind in his work. It was more a case of plain obstinacy than being unable to work. He cared very little for me and you can believe that I held little regard for him. All other means proving ineffective, I told him his pending punishment would be to throw him into the dungeon. I gave him a week to catch up, but at the end of that time, he was behind more than ever. I kept my promise. Into the dungeon he went.

When the P. K. thought the man had been punished enough, he was brought out to work again. The strain and starvation of the dungeon had made him truly unfit for such hard labor. There was no shamming this time. I could see it in his face. Handing the sledge to him, I knelt down and held the spike for him to pound into the stone. Everyone in the shop stopped work. I rose and told them to mind their own business and get back to work. They did as they were told, but every time I knelt to hold the spike, they would all stop again. I warned them for the last time, and finally, we all worked in a steady fashion. The men had stopped work for they were afraid the fellow I was helping would hit me over the head with his sledge as I bent over before him. Of course, he didn't touch me. In two weeks, he had recovered his health and was ahead of schedule on his work load. I thought no more of the incident until several years later when this inmate came up and spoke to me just before he was leaving the prison for good.

"Mister Conyes, when I came here I had made up my mind I wouldn't work for anyone. Then, I worked for you. Know why? Because, when you saw I could work and wouldn't, you punished me. Then, when you found out I really couldn't work, you helped me. I want to thank you for all you have done for me, sir, and I shall never forget your little kindness which helped to make my prison life bearable."

Prisoners are human and not such "ape men" as they are often painted.

On December 10, 1881, Onofrano Manzano murdered a fellow convict, Charles Williams. This was only one of some famous prison murders. Williams had some words in the kitchen with Angelo Cornetta while they were peeling vegetables. Manzano sided with Cornetta and attacked Williams with a knife. Joe Coburn, the famous heavyweight prizefighter of his time, risked his own life to overpower Manzano after he fatally stabbed Williams.

Then, on December 31, 1881, in the same kitchen, Daniel Cash, who had just returned to Sing Sing after testifying against

Manzano in the Grand Jury room, was struck down with a knife by Cornetta. Daniel Cash died in just a few minutes. Twelve days later, Cornetta, locked up in a dark cell, slashed his throat with a broken piece of water pipe. But Dr. Hiram Barber, the prison surgeon, sewed him back up and he survived. However, Cornetta was convicted of the murder of Cash and hanged in White Plains on May 11, 1885. Manzano was also sentenced to be hanged, but he had a new trial and was given life imprisonment. For fear that he would be killed in Sing Sing, Warden Brush had Manzano moved to Clinton for safety.

Keeper Patrick Mackin had a narrow escape when John Barrett, a desperate fourth-term burglar, made a fearful lunge at him with a long knife on July 24, 1882. I saw the weapon Barrett drew behind the keeper's back and shouted in warning that the prisoner was drawing a knife. As the convict struck out, Mackin jumped to one side and escaped with a slight flesh wound. Barrett then fled to the prison foundry and tried to incite a mutiny of the convicts there. Surrounded by five keepers, he struck savagely at Keeper John J. Good with a long ram. Good, pulling out his revolver, shot the prisoner through the heart and killed him. That was the end of Mr. Barrett. The warden found that the keeper had fired in self-defense.

There were humorous violations of prison rules in addition to the more violent ones. In particular, there was a grand orgy on September 19, 1890. Michael Brown, a burglar serving ten years, keeled over completely intoxicated. Soon, several others who had been engaged in unloading a freight car filled with rag also became hopelessly intoxicated. Warden Brush ordered a hasty investigation, but all the culprits were either too drunk or too wise to talk. In spite of closed mouths, the source of alcohol was soon identified. In one corner of the car, a barrel of whiskey was discovered. When the train crew had switched the freight car into the prison, they were unaware, as was the prison department, that it also contained freight for another designee. The convicts had found the barrel of whiskey and in moments had tapped it. Some, not having tasted spirits for several years, seized the opportunity to imbibe. Once discovered, the whiskey barrel was quickly sealed up again and shipped out of the prison walls.

I shall never forget the arrival of James Coleman on January 10, 1884. Unmindful of the rigors of winter, he arrived at the prison shorn of everything but his underwear. Realizing that the state took all civilian clothes away from each prisoner before fitting him out in the ugly prison stripes, Coleman took off all his clothes in the train at the Grand Central Station and made a present of them to a friend who saw him safely off in the custody of the sheriff.

When George Hall arrived in the winter of 1886 to serve five years for the theft of a watch and diamond from David Kraus, a jeweler at Eighty-Six Park Row in Manhattan, he stoutly maintained his innocence and claimed that he had been "framed" by the police. We always keep a close watch on these "innocent" prisoners when

FIGURE 18. The visiting room c. 1916—without any partitions, keepers had to keep a close eye on the prisoners and their visitors. Photo courtesy of Michael DeVall.

they receive callers in the visiting room. Here, it was discovered that Hall had a diamond concealed in one of his teeth. David Kraus was sent for and identified the diamond at the prison. Hall had offered it to a "lifer" in payment for sugar and tea.

Later, I saw Joshua G. Many, an innocent man, "locked up" within the walls on August 22, 1899, by an overzealous keeper. With the aid of prison attendants, he vainly tried to get the keeper to release him. Keeper John Kelly had allowed Many to drive in the side gate with a team of horses. Kelly had orders not to let anyone in or out of that exit except with a pass. When Many got a load of stone and started to drive out, Kelly, from the watchtower, refused to let him go. He insisted that Many would have to get Warden Johnson's permission to open the gate, but Johnson was out of town.

When other prison officials protested that Many had a pass to enter, Kelly retorted, "Yes, but he has none to get out." The keeper said that a prisoner had escaped that way a short time before. He wasn't going to take any chances. Deputy Ward Travis, who had also been absent, was located and summoned to the prison. He persuaded Kelly to open the gate, so Many and his horses were eventually "discharged."

I worked a murderer in the stone shed by the name of Hackett. He did his work well enough, but I could see it was a hard strain for him. One day, he came up to me and said, "Mr. Conyes, this work is too much for me. I'm a clerical man and have never done any heavy work before. I wish you would transfer me to some other place."

"Well, Hackett," I replied, "I can't change your work assignment because that authority rests with the warden. You've been a good man. Why don't you write to him yourself and tell him about it?"

"I would, sir," replied Hackett, "but I have no pencil or paper. They won't let us have any now."

He was right, so I said, "Go to my desk. You'll find pencil and paper there. Write your letter and hurry back. I'll see that it reaches the warden. Go on now and stop staring at me."

A few days later, Hackett was transferred to the library, where he worked for the next twenty years. At the expiration of that time, he came up for parole. I was in the "state" (tailor) shop then. Hackett came in a few days before his departure to be fitted for civilian clothes.

When he saw me, he hurried up and exclaimed, "Why, Mr. Conyes, you'll never know how glad I am to be going home. It's been a long time and you've been splendid to me. I shall never forget how you allowed me to go to your desk and write a letter to the warden. I'll see you again in a few days—on my way out."

The incident had escaped my mind, but I recognized him when he spoke of the letter. It just so happened, he was to be released one day too late for an overcoat, so I sent to see the warden. He told me that I should know what to do about it, and I did. When Hackett was ready to leave, I placed a bundle containing the overcoat into his hands. I didn't dare put it on him because of the rules, and told him not to open the package until he had arrived home. A few days later, I received a letter from him in which he had written over four pages of thanks. Hackett has never forgotten me, nor I him.

Another well-remembered incident at Sing Sing is that of the "One-Eyed Marksman." On the afternoon of January 15, 1881, Frank, alias "Bucky" Walsh and two other inmates tried to gain their freedom by rushing between the guard posts. They hoped to be able to get across the Hudson River, which was frozen at the time. The guards on pit duty spied Walsh making his mad dash for the river and ordered him to stop. His companions turned back; however, Walsh increased his speed and kept heading for the ice, which looked so good to him as an avenue of escape. The guards, with the exception of Keeper Nolan, who had one good eye, opened fire upon the fugitive. When asked by the sergeant of the guard why he wasn't firing, Nolan replied that he had but one eye.

"Hell!" bellowed the sergeant. "That's enough to aim with."

Nolan obeyed orders. The first shot from his rifle drilled Walsh through the heart and he died in his tracks. The incident preyed on Nolan's mind and, it is said, led to his death soon after.

I served in the stone shed for twelve years. While there, I supervised the cutting of all stone used in building the wall along the road from the Ossining depot to the village. The stone for the new mess hall was also cut in my shed. I supervised the construction of this

FIGURE 19. The cutting of the stone used in building the wall from the Ossining Depot to the Village of Ossining was supervised by Alfred Conyes in the stone shed at Sing Sing Prison. Photo courtesy of the Ossining Historical Society.

building from 1892 until its completion in 1897. During this time, I submitted plans to the warden for some larger windows in the old cell block. The small ones were never opened and the sunlight barely managed to creep through them. The warden gave his consent and now the inmates have plenty of sunlight and fresh air.

In addition, the prisoners under my charge built the old death house. Thomas Pallister was one of the gang on this job. He had killed a policeman and was sentenced to the chair. I shall explain later how he managed his escape, but the getaway was made possible because of his thorough knowledge of the building. Charles

FIGURE 20. Conyes submitted plans for larger windows to be installed in the old cell block. His plans were approved and the larger windows provided sorely needed fresh air and sunlight for the prisoners. Photo courtesy of Ossining Historical Society.

McElvaine was another. He was sentenced for killing a grocer in Queens—the first man in the world to be sent to the chair. However, because of delays through appeals, he was not the first to die by electric current. His death occurred in February 1892.

After working a dozen years in the stone shed, the dust had begun to settle in my lungs and the doctor advised me to change my position before more serious complications set in. There were no other keepers to take my place, and eventually, the stone contract was abandoned.

To Be Put to Death

On June 4, 1888, Governor Hill signed the bill which abolished hanging for all murders committed after January 1, 1889, substituting death by electricity. The bill was the outcome of a recommendation contained in the first annual message of Governor Hill to the State Legislature in 1885, being as follows:

> The present mode of executing criminals by hanging has come down to us from the Dark Ages and it may well be questioned whether the science of the modern day cannot provide a means for taking the life of such as are condemned to die in a less barbarous manner. I commend this suggestion to the consideration of the Legislature.[1]

The attention of scientific men was attracted to the subject by this message, and in 1886, the Gerry Commission was appointed by the Legislature to "investigate and report the most humane and practical method of carrying into effect the sentence of death in capital cases."[2]

The bill consisted of elaborate and carefully drawn amendments to the Code of Criminal Procedure. It stated that the prisoner sentenced to death should be immediately conveyed by the sheriff to one of the state prisons and be kept there in solitary confinement until the day of execution, to be visited only by officers, his relatives, physician, clergymen, and counsel. The court imposing sentence should name merely the week within the execution was to take place. The particular day within such week was left to the discretion of the principal officer of the prison. The execution was required to be practically private. Only officials, clergymen, physicians, and a limited number of citizens would be allowed to be present. After the execution, funeral services could be held within the prison walls and the body could be delivered into the custody of a relative, if requested. Otherwise, it should be decently interred within the prison grounds.

As soon as this law received the signature of the governor, it began to be generally discussed and criticized. Differing views were taken by prominent electricians. Numerous experiments were conducted by Harold P. Brown, an electrician of New York City, all tending to show the especially fatal force of the alternating current. With a current of 1500 volts, he declared that there could not be the slightest doubt of instantaneous death. The Westinghouse Electric Company, which had secured the rights of Nikola Tesla's patent of the alternating current system, entered into a bitter controversy with Mr. Brown. There had been opposition to the alternating current because of concerns about its safety and potential health hazard. The use of the alternating current for electrocutions only fueled public concern. Brown, however, went on with his experiments and finally made a contract with the state to furnish its killing apparatus. He furnished three Westinghouse dynamos.

William Kemmler, of Buffalo, N.Y., was the first man to become the legal victim of electrical execution. The crime for which he was sentenced was committed on the night of March 28, 1889, in the poverty-stricken apartments in Buffalo occupied by Kemmler and Tillie Zeigler, the woman who passed as his wife. Kemmler came home late at night, drunk and quarrelsome. Tillie was in the same condition. The quarrel that sprang up was brought to an abrupt end when Kemmler seized a hatchet and struck her down. He was caught in the act and expressed no penitence for the deed, remarking that his victim deserved to be killed.

The trial for the murder began on May 6, 1889, before Judge Childs and ended four days later in Kemmler's conviction. Judge Childs sentenced Kemmler to execution by electricity in the state prison at Auburn during the week beginning June 24, 1889. At once, the prisoner's counsel came to the conclusion that the mode of executing the death penalty prescribed by the new law was cruel and unusual, and therefore unconstitutional. He took an exception to the sentence, which was overruled a few days later, and the death warrant signed. Kemmler became an inmate of Auburn Prison on May 18, 1889.

Two weeks before the beginning of the week during which Kemmler was to be executed, a notice of appeal to the General Term was served. Warden Durston was required, by a writ of habeas corpus, to produce the murderer before County Judge Day on June 20 and show cause why he should not be released on the ground that the law under which he was sentenced was unconstitutional. Warden Durston produced the prisoner on the day named, but the hearing was adjourned until June 25.

At this point in the proceedings, there began a stubborn and skillful fight to prevent Kemmler from being executed. W. Bourke Cockran came forward as his counsel, although nobody imagined that he was retained by Kemmler or anyone who, through feeling sympathetic for the poor wretch himself, desired that he should escape punishment for his crime. It was generally believed that Mr. Cockran was retained by the Westinghouse Electric Company to do everything possible to prevent Kemmler from being the means of proving the truth or falsehood of Mr. Brown's claims.

As time for the first testing of their alternate current system as a death agent approached, the Westinghouse Electric Company became more and more anxious that it should not be tested. Mr. Cockran appeared before Judge Day and urged that the new law was "cruel, unusual, and unconstitutional." Judge Day appointed a referee to take testimony. During the reference in Mr. Cockran's office, dozens of experts were cross-examined. The testimony was laid before Judge

Day, who, early in October 1889, declared the law constitutional. This decision was affirmed by the General Term on December 20, 1889, and by the Court of Appeals on April 21, 1890.

Kemmler was again sentenced to death. After the preparations for his execution had been completed, Roger Sherman of New York obtained, in a mysterious manner, a writ of habeas corpus from Judge Wallace of the United States Circuit Court as a stay to allow application for writ of error to be made to the United States Supreme Court. This application was denied on May 23. Kemmler was sentenced once more, and after a futile attempt to replevin the state's electrical apparatus, those who were so desirous that he should not be killed by electricity were obliged to give up.

The execution of Kemmler, which took place on August 6, 1890, was a most revolting affair and may best be ascertained by the following newspaper account:

> A sacrifice to the whims and theories of the coterie of cranks and politicians who induced the Legislature of this State to pass a law supplanting hanging by electrical execution was offered to-day in the person of William Kemmler, the Buffalo murderer. He died this morning under the most revolting circumstances, and with his death there was placed to the discredit of the State of New-York an execution that was a disgrace to civilization.
>
> Probably no convicted murderer of modern times has been made to suffer as Kemmler suffered. Unfortunate enough to be the first man convicted after the passage of the new execution law, his life has been used as the bone of contention between the alleged humanitarians who supported the law, on one side, and the electric-light interests, who hated to see the commodity in which they deal reduced to such a use as that. . . .
>
> The execution cannot merely be characterized as unsuccessful. It was so terrible that the word fails to convey the idea.

[Among] . . . those who accepted the invitation of the Warden to witness Kemmler's death [were]: Dr. E. C. Spitzka, Dr. George F. Shrady, Dr. Carlos F. MacDonald, . . . all of New York; . . . District Attorney George P. Quimby of Buffalo, . . . Joseph C. Veiling, Deputy Sheriff of Erie County; . . . [and] the Rev. Horatio Yates, Chaplain of the Auburn Prison. . . .

. . .

In the meantime Warden Durston had arisen and had gone to the cell of the condemned man. He carried with him the death warrant, and he read it to Kemmler as the latter sat on the side of his bunk. Kemmler's sole remark when the Warden had finished reading was: "All right, I am ready." The warden then left the cell, and in the entrance hall above met the witnesses who had accepted his invitation. While most of the visitors loitered about the hall, Warden Durston went with J. C. Veiling, Kemmler's old Buffalo keeper, to the murderer's cell. Kemmler was apparently greatly pleased to see Veiling, and insisted that he should remain to breakfast with him. To this proposition Veiling assented, and a good breakfast was soon set before them. . . .

After the meal Kemmler was asked if he had any objection to having his hair cut, and he said he had not. Veiling therefore produced a pair of shears and cut the hair from the murderer's head. Kemmler sat smiling while the shears were being plied. Veiling was very nervous, and made a sorry job of the haircutting. When he had finished his work, the crown of Kemmler's head . . . had the appearance of a great scar.

Several times the murderer addressed Veiling. "They say I am afraid to die," he said, "but they will find that I ain't. I want you to stay right by me, Joe, and see me through this thing and I will promise you that I won't make any trouble."

. . .

After [Kemmler] had crossed the threshold [of the death chamber], there was, for an instant, the deadest silence. It was broken by Warden Durston:

"Gentlemen," he said, "this is William Kemmler." And Kemmler bowed.

"Gentlemen," he said, "I wish you all good luck. I believe I am going to a good place, and I am ready to go. I want only to say that a great deal has been said about me that is untrue. I am bad enough. It is cruel to make me out worse."

As he finished this little speech, he bowed again, and was about to sit down in a chair which had been placed beside the death chair. Warden Durston, seeing this, stepped forward, and Kemmler, noticing his action, saw that the time had come, and instead of sitting where he had intended, turned and easily dropped into the seat. Still he did it much as one might after a long walk fall into the welcome arms of an easy chair. He sat with the light from the window streaming full on his face, and immediately in front of him was the semicircle of witnesses. Warden Durston stepped to the chair, and at his request Kemmler arose. It was desired to see whether his clothing had been so cut away at the base of the spine as to allow of a clean contact between the electrode and the flesh. It was found that the outer garments had been cut, but the lower clothing had not been so. Durston took out a pocket knife and cut two small triangular pieces out of the shirt.

Then Kemmler easily settled back into the chair again. As he did so Durston started to get the rear piece in position. A murmur of surprise passed among the witnesses when Kemmler turned calmly to the Warden and in such tones as one might speak to a barber who was shaving him, said calmly: "Now take your time and do it all right, Warden. There is no rush. I don't want to take any chances on this thing, you know."

"All right, William," answered Durston, and then began to adjust the headpiece. It looked horrible with its leather bands crossing the doomed man's forehead and chin and partially concealing his features. When the job was finished Durston stepped back. Kemmler shook his head as one might when trying on a new hat, and then just as coolly as before said: "Warden, just make that a little tighter. We want everything all right, you know."

The warden did as requested and then started to fix the straps around the body, arms, and legs. There were eleven of them. As each was buckled, Kemmler would put some strain on it so as to see if it was tight enough. All appeared to suit him, and in answer to a question by the warden, he answered, "All right." Durston then stepped to the door. The last minute had come.

THE FATAL CURRENT TURNED ON.

Standing on the threshold he turned and said quietly, "Is all ready?" Nobody spoke. Kemmler merely lifted his eyes and for a moment turned them enough to catch a glimpse of the bright, warm sunlight that was streaming through the window of the death chamber.

"Good-bye, William," said Durston, and a click was heard. The "good-bye" was the signal to the men at the lever. The great experiment of electrical execution had been launched. New-York State had thrown off forever the barbarities, the inhumanities of hanging its criminals. But had it? Words will not keep pace with what followed. Simultaneously with the click of the lever the body of the man in the chair straightened. Every muscle of it seemed to be drawn to its highest tension. It seemed as though it might have been thrown across the chamber were it not for the straps which held it. There was no movement of the eyes. The body was as rigid as though cast in bronze, save for the index finger of the right hand, which closed up so tightly that the nail penetrated the flesh on the first joint, and the blood trickled out on the arm of the chair.

Drs. Spitzka and Macdonald stood in front of the chair, closely watching the dead or dying man. Beside them was Dr. Daniels, holding a stop-watch.

After the first convulsion there was not the slightest movement of Kemmler's body. An ashen pallor had overspread his features. Five seconds passed, ten seconds, fifteen seconds, sixteen, and seventeen. It was just 6:43 o'clock. Dr. Spitzka, shaking his head, said: "He is dead." Warden Durston pressed the signal button and at once the dynamo was stopped. The assembled witnesses who had sat as still as mutes up to this point gave breath to a sigh. The great strain was over. Then the eyes that had been momentarily turned from Kemmler's body returned to it and gazed with horror on what they saw. The men rose from their chairs impulsively and groaned at the agony they felt. "Great God! he is alive!" someone said; "Turn on the current," said another; "See he breathes," said a third; "For God's sake kill him and have it over," said a representative of one of the press associations, and then, unable to bear the strain, he fell on the floor in a dead faint. District Attorney Quimby groaned audibly and rushed from the room.

Drs. Spitzka and MacDonald stepped toward the chair. Warden Durston, who had started to loosen the electrode on the head, raised it slightly and then hastily screwed it back into place. Kemmler's body had become limp and settled down in the chair. His chest was raising and falling and there was a heavy breathing that was perceptible to all. Kemmler was, of course, entirely unconscious. Drs. Spitzka and Macdonald kept their wits about them. Hastily they examined the man, not touching him, however. Turning to Warden Durston, who had just finished getting the head electrode back in place, Dr. Spitzka said: "Have the current turned on again, quick—no delay." Durston sprang to the door, and in an instant had sounded the two bells, which informed the man at the lever that the current must be turned on.

THE CURRENT TURNED ON AGAIN.

Again came that click as before, and again the body of the unconscious wretch in the chair became as rigid as one of bronze. It was awful, and the witnesses were so horrified by the ghastly sight that they could not take their eyes off it. The dynamo did not seem to run smoothly. The current could be heard sharply snapping. Blood began to appear upon the face of the wretch in the chair. It stood on the face like sweat.

The capillary or small blood vessels under the skin were being ruptured. But there was worse than that. An awful odor began to permeate the death chamber, and then, as though to cap the climax of this fearful sight, it was seen that the hair under and around the electrode on the head and the flesh under and around the electrode at the base of the spine was singeing. The stench was unbearable.

How long this second execution lasted—for it was a second execution, if there was any real life in the body when the current was turned on for the second time—is not really known by anybody. Those who held watches were too much horrified to follow them. Some said afterward that it lasted a minute. One said it lasted fully four minutes and a half. Opinions ranged all the way between these figures. Dr. Spitzka, who was as cool as any man could be under such circumstances, says it was not more than a minute. It was 6:51 o'clock when the signal went to the man at the lever to shut off the current. Kemmler had been in the chair just eight minutes from the time the current was first turned on. There is nobody among the witnesses present who can tell just how much of that time the current was passing through the body of Kemmler.

As soon as the current was off again Warden Durston rapidly unscrewed the electrodes and unbuckled the straps. Kemmler's body again was limp. This time he was surely dead. There was no doubt of that. The body was left sitting upright in the chair, and the witnesses of the tragedy that had been enacted passed out into the stone corridors as miserable, as weak-kneed a lot of men as can be imagined. It had nauseated all but a few of them, and the sick ones had to be looked out for. They were all practically silent for some time. Their minds were too busy to enable them to talk. They all seemed to act as though they felt that they had taken part in a scene that would be told to the world as a public shame, as a legal crime.

. . .

Examination of the electrodes on the fatal chair discloses that the sponge at the base of the spine was scorched and dried by heat generated, owing to imperfect contact or to insufficient wetting of the sponge during contact. The result was a terrible burning of the back clear through to the spine. The skin in contact had been burned to a black cinder and the flesh above had been cooked until yellow, while the inner tissues had been baked.

The sponge in the upper electrode had been singed, though not so much as the other, and the scalp only singed instead of incinerated.[3]

The manner in which Kemmler was put to death caused no end of controversy. Cable dispatches were received from all parts of the world denouncing death by the electric current. A. P. Southwick, who had introduced the bill into the Legislature, was assailed on all sides. The president of the Westinghouse Electric Company expressed himself as satisfied that the people surely would not tolerate such a loathsome practice. The daily papers were full of controversy for and against. A few stood firm, and today, death by the electric chair is an established way for those sentenced to die to be put to death.

Capital punishment has been and, no doubt, will always be a source of the keenest argument. The infliction of the death penalty was declared by many to be terribly wrong, based upon the belief that if the fate of each human soul is fixed in this life, to determine his life by law is not merely the murder of the body, but the irrevocable ruin of the soul.

On the other hand, many believe that fear of the chair and the example set by it would curb the activities of the murderers. However, the chair has set very little example because of the provision in the law that all executions must be practically private. One rarely even sees the chair until he is to be executed in it. The greatest majority of the people know nothing about it, and because of that fact, little do they care.

Holding the Line

· ◆ ─────── ◆ ·

With the passage of the new execution law, it became necessary to construct a death house at Sing Sing. I was delegated to superintend the building of this structure, which was accomplished entirely by convict labor with the stone taken from the prison quarries. The building, situated at the south end of the prison, was 120 feet long and 30 feet wide and contained thirteen cells. These cells were somewhat larger than the regulation ones and had no other furniture in them but a bed.

The only exercise which the prisoners in these cells have is walking about in a yard surrounded by a stone wall twelve feet high and over a foot thick. The windows in the cell block are covered by heavy curtains which are always drawn to prevent outsiders from looking in. Once a condemned man is admitted to the death house, he is unable to see anything except the sky overhead.

The meals are somewhat better than the regular prison fare. It has been a popular belief that a condemned man may have whatever he desires for his final meal. This is true with limitations. His choice is confined to food available in Ossining.

Visitors were formerly allowed to stand right in front of the cell while a keeper stood by watching to see that nothing was passed

Wing in New Death House

FIGURE 21. Alfred Conyes supervised the building of the new death house. Photo courtesy of Guy Cheli.

from the visitor to the prisoner. The time allotted then, as now, was one hour. Visiting customs have been changed, and now when a condemned man has a visitor, he is taken from his cell and locked in a steel cage. Between him and his loved ones is a space of six feet or more and not a single screen, but two, with one being fine mesh.

On the day he is to die, the condemned man is taken from his cell about 8:30 in the morning. If he so desires, he may say good-bye to those in his corridor. He passes down a hall until he comes to a room in which there are half a dozen cells even larger than the one he previously occupied. He is bathed, shaved and dressed. His last hours are spent with loved ones or spiritual advisors. Men on their way to the chair are never given liquors or drugs at Sing Sing. As a general rule, very few show hysteria when they are brought to face the chair.

The chair itself is situated in a large room with plenty of light which comes through a skylight in the center of the ceiling. Directly under this is the killing apparatus. It looks much the same as a barber's chair.

The death chamber is always kept spotlessly clean. The floor is concrete and the walls white. In the rear are four benches where the witnesses sit. In front of them and to the right is a brown door with the one word "Silence" over it. This is the door through which the condemned man enters from his cell. To the left of the chair

FIGURE 22. The Sing Sing death chamber, where absolute silence was the rule. Photo courtesy of the Ossining Historical Society.

is a table covered with a white cloth and a door with glass panels. The electrician stands behind this door. He lays the tools needed in bringing about death on this table. The cloth is white so that he may see the tools quickly.

In another side room, directly to the left of the benches, there are three white-topped tables such as those used in hospital operating rooms. After the electricity has done its work, the body is brought into this room, where an autopsy is performed. The brain and other vital organs are removed. The body is then taken to the morgue, which adjoins the autopsy room. If it is not claimed by relatives, it is covered with quicklime and buried in the prison yard.

One of the most notable events of my career was the execution of the first men to die by the electric current at Sing Sing. Their deaths occurred on the night of July 7, 1891. Four men were sentenced to die and their executions caused quite a fuss after the Kemmler episode.

There was nothing in the life or character of any of them to excite sympathy. Their histories showed them to have largely lived in a "brute world" with practically no education.

James Slocum was, at one time, a baseball player, but drink made him unfit for almost any labor. On New Year's Eve night, 1889, he killed his wife in a little room of a Cherry Street apartment in New York City. An axe, covered with blood, was found near her. Slocum claimed, however, after his fate was practically sealed, that he struck her in a momentary passion with a pitcher. His claim mattered not and after a prompt conviction, he was sentenced to death by electrocution by Judge Martine in March, 1890.

Harris A. Smiler was a West Side rough. He had once been a lieutenant in the Salvation Army. Drink caused his ruin. He had married three wives without taking the trouble to procure a divorce from the first. Maggie Drainey was one of the wives, who because she could not bear his treatment, refused to live with him. In revenge, he shot her on April 13, 1889, at 284 Seventh Avenue, New York City.

Shibuya Jugiro, the "Jap," as he was called, was a sailor, who during a quarrel in a James Street boarding house in New York City stabbed Mura Commi. Roger Sherman, attorney for Jugiro, by taking advantages of the technicalities in the law, gained delays until all further chance was exhausted.

Joseph Wood, a Negro, was tried for shooting Charles Ruffian in a grocery store along the aqueduct where both worked. He was tried before Recorder Smyth and convicted by a jury. His lawyer claimed to have new evidence of self-defense in the case and did everything in his power to save the man, but to no avail.

The newspapers lost no time in criticizing the executions. Warden Brown had refused to admit reporters to witness the affair, and they assailed him on all sides.

> These executions are surrounded by an air of mystery and secrecy deeper than is warranted by any transaction that is legal. It looks on the face of things as if the queer coterie of influential cranks, scientific men, and politicians who created the electrical execution law are bound to have these executions go off to suit themselves. . . . Gov. Hill . . . has around him just the men who would see that his will is obeyed. They are here now, preparing to put to death four condemned murderers, and acting as though the whole matter was one of their own personal interest which did not concern the public in the slightest degree.
>
>   . . .
>
> The suggestion has been made several times to-day that if the Czar of Russia ever wants to put on a substitute to apply gags, to wield the knout, and to make still more absolute his despotic sway, he cannot do better than to give the job to Warden Brown, who has been showing samples of his ability to do the Czar's work within twenty-four hours.
>
> The Warden's conduct was peculiar. He was by no means weighed down by the awful responsibility which rested on his shoulders, and when about making his preparations to take the lives of four men, he tossed aside all dignity and seemed to revel in the luxury of playing tricks with the newspaper men.[1]

It was quite necessary that the details be kept out of the papers because of the unpleasant publicity caused by the Kemmler affair. The warden had orders not to let newspaper men within the prison walls. He ordered me to get a group of the guards together, arm them with rifles, and keep the crowd away from the prison entrance. He went out to the road, drew a line across the highway and told me to keep the crowd back of it, even if I had to shoot. Thereafter, the warden became known as "Deadline" Brown.

The orders were pretty strict and I didn't feel any too comfortable about carrying them out, but I told the crowd what the warden had said, and they stood back where they would be out of the way.

There were about fifty reporters there from New York papers. It was written:

> If they were Sioux Indians who had invaded a government military reservation with war paint and tomahawks, they might have expected the same treatment which Warden Brown gave them.
>
> About this time, several reporters wrote a note to Warden Brown asking if he would grant an interview either before or after the execution. A guard took it to the prison. A few moments later, Mr. Brown sent back the original note endorsed "declined and thanks." As it was being delivered to the men who had sent it, Warden Brown stood in the door of his office with a sneering laugh on his face. That is the kind of man he is.
>
> By private arrangement with the newspaper men, (the only concession he granted them), Warden Brown had settled that the news of the executions would be given them by a system of flag signals to be hoisted on the staff of the cupola of the prison. A color represented each one of the condemned men. When a flag was hoisted, those on the outside were to understand that the man represented by its color agreed upon was dead. To Slocum was given the white flag. To Smiler, the Salvation Army murderer, was

given the blue color. Wood, the Negro, was assigned the black flag by the warden, the assignment being accompanied by the characteristic witticism that "it was good enough for a coon." Jugiro, the "Jap," was represented by a red flag.[2]

The sunrise gun at the Peekskill camp, ten miles away, had just boomed forth when a white flag was seen going up the flag staff. "Slocum is dead" was the word passed along through the crowd which had gathered in front of me. They waited and watched until the blue flag was hoisted and the crowd knew that Smiler was dead. After a while, the black flag was seen to appear followed by the red. It was all over and the crowd began to disperse. One of the hardest duties of my prison experience was a thing of the past.

Every witness of the executions was made to pledge, in writing, never to reveal any detail of the executions unless requested to do so by the officials. The newspapers hinted that officials were fearful lest they should fail:

Governor Hill and his henchman, Warden Brown, made up their minds that these experiments with the law should not go before the public as anything else but successes and they packed the jury accordingly with picked men. Hill is an adept at picking juries if the people of Elmira and Chemung counties are to be believed.[3]

The last day of these four men on earth was spent very quietly. Smiler, the Salvation Army man, read his Bible and sang salvation hymns all day. Slocum and Wood often joined in the choruses and they would keep singing for hours. Slocum had been in confinement for so long, he appeared indifferent to the end. Wood, the Negro, had the sympathy of all—who believed that he had killed a man in self defense. Jugiro acted like a crazy man. Unable to understand English, the idea of the chair was associated in his mind as an end more awful than anything he knew. Consequently, he was possessed with a terrible dread. He had made up his mind to fight so desperately that his keepers would almost have to kill him in self-defense.

Slocum was the first to die. As the solemn procession passed into the death chamber, his head bowed. He was silent and stared fixedly straight ahead. He was dressed in a new black, diagonal coat with dark trousers, white shirt, turned down collar and black tie. He stepped readily into the chair and the attendants began to secure him immediately. Straps were passed across his chest, under the arms and tightened. Others were placed over the arms just over the wrists. These were strongly secured so that it would be impossible for any distorting movements to result. The legs were firmly strapped to the chair. Then, around the head, was carried the belts or bands across the face. One passed just over the upper lip while another crossed his beard. The head electrode, with its wet sponge, was placed into position against his forehead. After making a rent in his trouser leg, the lower electrode was fastened to the calf of Slocum's leg. The wires were attached to the electrodes, and Warden Brown was told that all was ready. The details had not taken over two minutes.

Giving one look at the chair, Warden Brown dropped his hand-kerchief. This was the sign to Mr. Davis, the electrician, to turn on the current, and in turn, to signal the executioner, to switch it into the chair and through the body of the victim.

A current of approximately 1,450 volts passed through Slocum's body and he died at once. Muscular contraction had not been strong nor had it shocked the eye witnesses. The time of the contact was about twenty-five seconds. The engine room was signaled and the dynamo stopped. His body was limp as the attendants loosened the straps and carried him into the autopsy room.

Smiler was next. He came into the room with scarcely a tremor singing a hymn in a low voice. He kept singing while the straps were being adjusted until the one over his face was put into position. His eyes were kept on the floor. There was a slight convulsion as the current passed through Smiler and his countenance turned pale. He was a man of nervous temperament, but his death had been easy.

Wood, being a Negro, with a thick skull and naturally great resistance powers, received a more powerful current—about 1,500 volts. He walked into the room unaided muttering psalms in a low voice. He gazed around while the attendants were doing their work, but closed his eyes and kept them closed after the strap had been fastened across his face. The current was kept on a few seconds longer, but death came as in the two preceding cases.

The powerful Jap, Jugiro, whose uncivilized ways had put him far beyond any companionship with his fellow prisoners, was the last to suffer the extreme penalty. He was on his good behavior, and contrary to expectations, offered no resistance. His dress was like that of the others and he made no sign that he knew anything of what was going on about him. Death came quickly. After he was dead and everyone supposed that he had died without a shadow of religious beliefs, it was learned that he had a spot in his heart softer than the rest. The Rev. Mr. Law, who had once been a missionary to Japan, had conversed with the Jap in his native tongue, preparing him to meet his death.

The four bodies were stretched out in a row in the autopsy room. They were in a natural position and the faces looked much the same as in real life. The eyes were partially opened. Particular attention was given to see if the flesh had been burned where it had come in contact with the electrodes. However, with the exception of a small spot on Slocum's forehead, there was scarcely the faintest shadow of discoloration.

Newspaper men were naturally prone to criticize the actions of the officials concerned in these executions. They rebelled at the refusal of Warden Brown to allow them into the death chamber. On the day following the happenings at Sing Sing, nearly every newspaper in the country ran an editorial protesting against such actions. The following from the *New York Times* was especially vehement:

The whole proceeding was deprived of the impressiveness and solemnity intended by the law and turned into a burlesque by Warden Brown's officiousness. If he had contented himself by refusing to give information and excluding from the prison all but the designated and selected witnesses, he would have done his full duty. What information others might give out was none of his business and he had no lawful right to bind any man to secrecy and the wonder is that reputable physicians, clergymen and other citizens would submit to any pledge from him. Newspapers are prohibited from publishing any details of the execution, but nobody is, by law, prohibited from giving them out, and the newspapers are quite capable of taking care of their own responsibility and liability in the premises, and need no protection from the prison officials. It is simply impossible to prevent the publication of what purports to be the details of these executions and it would be much better to permit authentic accounts to be given rather than leave them to the imagination and invention of irresponsible reporters, some of whom may circulate mischievous statements. The result at Sing Sing yesterday seems to have demonstrated the entire success of executing the death penalty by the electric current; the utter folly of the provision of the law prohibiting the publication of the details and the peculiar unfitness of Warden Brown for any public duty requiring tact, good sense, and a decent regard for the rights of law-abiding citizens.[4]

After the controversy had calmed down, events at Sing Sing took on a quiet tone. I continued working in the stone shed, and with the exception of detecting one man who was trying to get away in one of the shipping cases, little occurred to bother me.

However, on August 23, 1892, Charles T. Vincent and James Welsh made one of the most sensational attempts to escape in the history of Sing Sing. Their attempted escape resulted in the death of Vincent. Welsh was recaptured after he had managed to get outside of the prison walls.

Vincent was twenty-six years old. He had lived in Hoboken, New Jersey, and was a long-term prisoner, having been sent up for

FIGURE 23. Vincent and Welsh occupied a cell on the third tier of the old cell block. Photo courtesy of Michael DeVall.

sixteen years for his assault and robbery of Thomas MacDonald of Brooklyn. He was serving his second term at Sing Sing and had also been in the penitentiary on Blackwell's Island.

Welsh was twenty-seven years of age. He was sent to prison from New York City on March 11, 1891, to serve five years for larceny.

The two men occupied the same cell, No. 883, on Gallery 17, which was the third tier above the corridor in the old cell block at the south end of the prison near the main door. Their cell was one of the closest in the prison to the office of Warden Brown.

Welsh was a skillful machinist, but was not employed at his trade at Sing Sing. Vincent and he worked in the tailor shop. They had occupied the same cell for only a few weeks. They managed to get several articles into their cell without being detected by the guards. These included two small cold chisels, one triangular file, two small files, one flat and the other round and both ground so that they might be used as drills, a large pair of shears, a piece of cloth, a nine-inch steel drill, a jackscrew, a small piece of mirror, two suits of plain clothes from the tailor shop, two pieces of board, some rope, and an iron lever. How the convicts got these things into their cell is still a mystery, but it may be reasonably assumed that they had the help of other prisoners who were aware that they were to attempt an escape.

They began operations at three o'clock on Sunday afternoon, two days prior to the attempt, by dismantling the lock on their cell. The lock and the lower half of the door were covered with two plates of sheet iron about a sixteenth of an inch thick. With their steel drill, they bored a hole in the sheet iron large enough to admit the point of the shears. Then, they cut away the sheet iron until they had the lock exposed. They bored holes into the lock until it was so torn that they could move back the cell door bolt.

According to Welsh, it took the convicts six hours to get the door open. They used the cloth to deaden the sound of the drilling and cutting so noise wouldn't reach the guards. They used the mirror to show them the approach of a guard, and when the glass showed that a guard was near, they stopped working. They were aware that one of the guards started from the bottom gallery and the other from the top, and that after the two drew near their cell and then off again, which was about every twenty minutes, the danger of detection was over for the time being.

After the men had managed to get their door open, they took the two pieces of board and bound them together with the rope. The board was to be laid from the rail of the gallery opposite their cell to the window sill across the corridor from which they were to make their escape.

They waited until 1:30 A.M. on Tuesday to make their escape. They doffed their prison suits and put on the clothing they had smuggled into their cell.

Vincent, a powerful man about six feet tall, was the first to leave the cell. He carried the board, which he placed across the corridor with the ends resting on the small window sill and the iron railing of the gallery. Then, he crawled along the board to the window and, taking the jackscrew from his pocket, fitted it into the rivet where the two bars crossed and worked the screw until he broke the rivet and separated the bars. He slipped the lever into the jackscrew and used it to force the upright bar aside. When he had pushed the bar over against the window casing, he crawled back into the cell and told Welsh to make his escape.

Welsh was slight and wiry, and the plan was to have him leave the prison first. After he dropped from the window, Vincent was to remove the board to the cell until the guard had passed, then replace it and make his escape.

Welsh crossed the board and started to go through the window, shoulders first. Vincent removed the board and was sneaking back to the cell with it when Guard Solomon Post discovered both men.

Post called to Vincent to throw up his arms. The convict shouted back that he would surrender. By this time, Welsh had squeezed through the window bars, dropped twenty feet onto a roof, and jumped into Warden Brown's flower bed in the front yard of the prison.

The guard hurried along the gallery until he was close to Vincent, who had put the board back from the railing to the window sill. Post had his revolver in his hand and ordered Vincent to go with him.

Vincent allowed the guard to approach within arm's length before he sprang upon him. Post managed to fire his revolver, but that was all he was able to do toward preventing the escape of Vincent. Post was a big man, but he proved no match for Vincent, who got the first finger of Post's left hand in his mouth, biting it nearly off while he grasped the other with both hands.

Vincent bent the guard over the gallery railing in an attempt to throw him sixty feet below. In this he failed, but in the struggle, he wrestled the revolver from the guard, who then called loudly for assistance. As soon as Vincent had possession of the revolver, he released his teeth from Post's finger and ran across the board to the window.

Guards James E. McCormick and Peter Short went into the encounter at this point. McCormick was on the ground floor when he heard the shot fired on the third tier. By the time he reached there, Vincent was crossing the board. McCormick shouted for him to stop, at which the convict fired at him. McCormick then shot several times at Vincent, who returned the fire.

While Vincent and McCormick were exchanging shots, the latter was joined by Short, who had been on the top gallery at the north end of the prison—more than a thousand feet away—when he heard the first shot. When he reached Gallery 17, he saw Vincent on the board with a pistol in his hand. He called to him to give up the revolver, but the convict fired at him and kept on across the board. When Vincent reached the window, Short fired several shots at him.

Vincent tried to squeeze through the window, all the time firing at the guards who stood on the gallery not more than ten feet away. At least fourteen shots were fired at Vincent, but only two struck him.

Vincent's size prevented him from getting through the window and he finally sat still there with a bullet through his right lung. He was dead before anyone could reach him. It was not known which of the guards fired the fatal shot as all of the firing was done in the dark. Vincent used his pistol while there was a charge left and the position in which he was found wedged in the window showed that he had made a desperate attempt to get through the bars while the bullets were rattling about his head.

The capture of Welsh was made by Keeper John P. Glynn. He was at lunch in the key room when he heard the firing. He thought the whole gallery was unlocked and that all the prisoners were loose. Fearing an outbreak, he did not dare to open the main door, and so he went into the prison yard to see what he could learn. As he stepped into the yard, he saw Welsh on the roof of one of the prison offices. He ordered the man to halt, but Welsh ran to the adjoining roof and jumped to the ground.

Welsh ran over the flower beds in front of the prison, Glynn in pursuit. When the convict had gone half the length of the prison, Glynn overtook him and both fell into a pit next to the prison wall. While they struggled in the pit, Glynn fired his revolver, but missed the convict.

Then Glynn drew his club and struck Welsh once or twice on the head, but the wiry young fellow broke away and ran like a deer toward the end of the prison. Glynn followed, firing as he ran. Welsh passed through the aperture next to the big iron gate with Glynn close on his heels. He started up the hillside over the railroad tunnel when a bullet from Glynn's revolver pierced his right shin.

Welsh stopped, exclaiming, "For God's sake, don't shoot again. I'm wounded."

Glynn ran up with his revolver aimed at the man's head and ordered him to throw up his arms. This he did, and Glynn made him walk back to the prison in that position, covering him with his revolver all the way.

By the time Glynn entered the prison office with Welsh, Warden Brown and P. K. Connaughton had been aroused and were about to enter the prison. The warden left Glynn with Welsh in his office, telling the keeper to shoot the convict dead if he moved.

Brown, Connaughton, and half a dozen keepers, armed with rifles, entered the cell block. Guards were hurrying everywhere about the corridor and great excitement prevailed. The prisoners were shouting at the tops of their voices and kicking on the doors of their cells. Brown and Connaughton ran along the gallery, calling to the prisoners that they would put bullets in them if they did not keep quiet. It was fully ten minutes before order was restored.

When Welsh returned on one of his later bits, it happened that I was present when he came in and inquired as to how his leg was feeling. He replied, "Captain, I've still got the damn bullet with me" and laughed heartily. One more conviction of a felony will mean a sentence of natural life under the Baumes Laws. I wonder if he will ever come back to stay.

The High Cost of Freedom

Leaving Sing Sing, Leaving this Earth

Just about eight months after the Vincent and Welsh break, on April 21, 1893, the first escape was made from the death house. Thomas Pallister and Frank Roehl, murderers sentenced to the chair, climbed out of prison, leaving a pair of keepers bound and gagged in their cells. The story of their escape rivals any fiction. These two men, under close watch and in solitary confinement, overpowered their armed guards, shoved them into the cells, and left them so helpless, all through the night, they were unable to sound the alarm. Everyone in the death house might have made an escape, but the others refused to leave.

There were five men occupying cells in this building awaiting death by the electric current. In one corridor were eight condemned cells. Cells 1, 6, and 7 were vacant. Pallister was in 2, Roehl in 3, Osmond in 4, Geoghegan in 5, and Carlyle W. Harris in 8.

The prison closed for the day on Thursday afternoon at about five o'clock. Guard James H. Hulse went into the death house to relieve the keeper on duty. Later in the evening, he was to be joined by Guard James W. Murphy.

Hulse nodded as usual in greeting the condemned men. He made the necessary inspection to see that everything was all right with both the cells and men. Then he took his seat for the night watch.

The evening meal, consisting of a platter of meat and pan of milk, had just been taken to the prisoners. Roehl's portion had become cold, and he asked Guard Hulse if it might be warmed on the stove. The request was granted and at about 7:30 P.M., the food was steaming. Roehl asked for his food, and Hulse carried the dishes over to his cell.

The dishes were of plain tin and too large to pass between the bars. Hulse unlocked and opened the prisoner's door to hand him the food. Immediately, Roehl threw black pepper into Hulse's eyes and seized him by the throat with both hands almost strangling him to death. In agony from the burning of his eyes, Hulse put up little resistance, and Roehl quickly backed him to the bars of Pallister's cell. Pallister seized the guard's arms and hands, holding him while Roehl relieved him of his revolver. Holding it at the guard's head, Roehl told him to march. Blinded by the pepper, Hulse was pushed into the cell which Roehl had just vacated. The convict shut the door and quickly turned the key in the lock, making Hulse a prisoner. He was told to remain there perfectly quiet and not make any attempt to give an alarm if he valued his life. Hulse obeyed the order implicitly for he never opened his mouth.

Roehl took the bunch of keys from the lock and went to Pallister's cell, which he quickly unlocked, and let his fellow inmate out. The two then went to the other cells and told the three men behind the bars that they had locked the guard up and were going to break out of the prison. When asked if they cared to go along, all three refused to take the chance. Carlyle Harris was appealed to, but he refused, telling the men that they were in bad business.

Roehl and Pallister, who now had complete control of the room, made preparations for a hasty departure. They were aware that Guard Murphy would not be around until nine o'clock, so they had a bit over an hour in which to cut their way out.

They took the iron poker from under the stove. It was about a foot and a half long and well adapted for use as a jimmy. Next, they grabbed the round-cornered shovel and climbed to the top of the cells. As noted earlier, Tommy Pallister had worked under me on this building, and his thorough knowledge of its construction put him in good stead. Only a few knew of the trap door on the roof of the death house. Pallister managed to open the trap door, and the two men took turns attacking the flimsy roof about two feet above. It was composed of light timbers and boards covered with some tarred paper and gravel.

After they had cut a hole in the roof large enough to escape, they dropped back into the corridor to wait for Murphy. They knew if they could secure him as they had Hulse, they would have the entire night to make distance between themselves and the prison walls. If they had left at once, Murphy would have discovered the plot, and they would be followed in less than a half an hour.

FIGURE 24. Roehl and Pallister were able to escape through the roof of the death house because of Pallister's knowledge of a trap door. Photo courtesy of Michael DeVall.

These two men knew what they were doing. They lay in wait for Murphy. While listening for his approach, Roehl saw the day keeper's hat and took it for himself after tearing off the gold-lettered word "Keeper." Pallister, after having taken Hulse's shoes, which happened to fit him, obtained an old derby hat which had been hanging on a peg in back of the stove. Both were in the citizen's clothes which are supplied to condemned men on their reception at the death house. Thus, they were effectively disguised as far as clothing was concerned.

Murphy appeared at nine o'clock. Pallister and Roehl let him into the room and quickly slammed the heavy, iron-bound, oak door shut. They quickly pounced upon him and, after taking away his pistol, bound and thrust him into cell 2, which Pallister had previously occupied.

As soon as Murphy had been locked up, they hoisted themselves through the hole they had made in the roof and easily dropped to the ground. They crept cautiously across a short distance of the prison yard and scaled the twelve foot wall to freedom. This wall was not guarded after the convicts had been locked in their cells at night, so the men had little difficulty in clambering over it without being seen.

In the morning, the relief guards found Hulse and Murphy trussed up in the cells. The eyes of Hulse were highly inflamed from the pepper. Word of the escape was sent out from the prison in an early alarm. It created great excitement, and as the details came out, furnished the most sensational topic of the day. Footprints were found near the edge of the Hudson River showing where the escaped men had shoved off in a small boat.

Officials were quite outspoken in condemning the carelessness which made the escape possible. At the district attorney's office in New York City, suspicions of the statements reported from Sing Sing were freely uttered.

The search for the missing men was continued for several weeks until their bodies, riddled with bullets, were found lying on the shore of the river about five miles south of the prison. No one knew who fired the shots. Their fate remains a mystery.

Carlyle Harris, who refused to go with Pallister and Roehl, was executed on May 8, 1893. His case was one of the most notorious in the history of the state, and his losing battle for freedom was most dramatic. Nearly everyone concerned believed Harris to be innocent, but there was no help for him. His trial brought about one of the largest demonstrations in the history of New York City. He had been convicted of poisoning his secret bride, Helen Potts.

Harris made the final appeal for his life before Recorder Frederick Smyth in the Court of General Sessions on March 20, 1893. He was a man of intellectual ability and one of the most dignified ever to appear before the bar.

At 9:30 o'clock, Harris was taken from his cell in the Tombs and manacled to Keepers Brown and Burke. He had been very sick all morning with nausea. He was ghastly pale and shook like a man with the ague, but walked with his head erect. He went out of the Franklin Street exit of the Tombs and seemed rather frightened at the large crowd that had gathered there.

To avoid the throng that had filled Centre Street, the wretched man was rushed up Elm Street to Reade, through the building of the Department of Public Works, and thence across Chambers Street into the court. As he ran across Chambers Street through a passage in the crowd which the police had kept open, there was a roar from the thousands of people who gathered there . . .

In spite of the care which had been ordered in admitting people to the courtroom, the place was crowded to suffocation. Only about a dozen women were there and they appeared to be women of refinement . . .[1]

The recorder started promptly at ten o'clock. After Harris had been called to the bar, District Attorney Nicoll asked the court to fix the date for the execution of the sentence of death. The motion for a new trial had been denied, and the district attorney was anxious to bring the case to a close. The clerk of court asked Harris if he had anything to say.

Harris pulled himself together; he thanked the court for its courtesy and launched into a speech which lasted for a full hour and a half. He went fully into every detail and talked as though he were arguing a case rather than pleading with the one man who had the power to name the date for his execution. He was quite weak and saved himself from collapse by frequent drinks of brandy and water.

Harris took the district attorney to task for having made a statement that the Court of Appeals had gone out of its way to confirm the conviction of the lower court in his case by expressing its entire confidence in the proof of his guilt, and the further statement made, he declared, before the affidavits had been submitted, that the recorder would deny a motion for a new trial.

> Then Harris said that he understood that as soon as sentence had been passed upon him he was to be railroaded to Sing Sing. He asked that the Recorder would allow him two or three days after sentence in the Tombs so that he might arrange his affairs and in which he might dictate a short biography of his life, to be printed and sold for his mother's benefit . . .
>
> Dilworth Choate, who did much in the working up of the Harris case for the District Attorney's office and who will be remembered as the man who served a term of imprisonment because he was caught concealed in the Flack jury room, next received the attention of Harris.
>
> "Sneak Choate" he called him, and he referred to the whole case as the triumph of Choate over justice. He recited that Choate, "a gabbler for a disreputable sheet," worked up the whole case against him for the sake of getting promotion from his employer.
>
> Tracing the progress of the charge and the publicity given to the alleged murder of his wife, Harris told how he at once went to District Attorney Nicoll and surrendered himself, offering bail. He was told then that there were no charges against him and he went home, but only after the District Attorney had assured him that he would investigate the charges. Harris said that "Sneak Choate" from that day on kept writing sensational articles about him, in which he accused him of at least three murders, two of persons

whom he never met; twenty abortions, bigamy, larceny, rape, and forgery.

. . . (Harris) was very bitter against (Assistant District Attorney) Wellman, who was sitting just in front of him. . . .

"There arose a public clamor," said Harris, "asking why a boy, young and gently nurtured, should murder a girl who was beautiful, who loved him, who would have enriched him, whose family had offered to further his professional ambitions. But Mr. Wellman was equal to the emergency. He sprang into the breach, throwing out to the world a bombshell of official utterance through the columns of the press, that he had found my former wife, and that her name was Lulu Van Zandt. I married her, he said, in 1883. So, your Honor, the last tie of sympathy which bound me to my race was broken.

"I will never forget the morning that the members of the press came to me, the morning the story was published. I told them the story was a lie, and they proved it so, God bless them. They found the certificates of my birth and baptism, and they found those of Miss Lulu Van Zandt, and they proved that in 1883 I was a boy in knickerbockers and she was an infant in small clothes, and we had never met each other in our lives. And they proved that Wellman lied.

"Is there a human creature more vile than the abandoned woman who walks the slums? There is. It is a minister of justice who prostitutes his official utterance for the furtherance of a personal ambition or the gratification of a private spite. You may be surprised that I have dared to speak this way about those who are officers of this court, but, your Honor, it is not blackguardism. Every word I have said I have said only because I honestly believed it. I speak for the last time. I cannot afford to state untruths to-day.

"Isn't it strange, your Honor, that I, brought here to be sentenced to a disgraceful death, can look down from a pedestal of just contempt upon certain of those who have encompassed this end?"[2]

Harris had become imbued with the idea that he was a martyr and that the record of his case would be a monument to injustice. He seemed to believe that all the world considered him innocent of the crime except those directly interested in the prosecution.

Harris began to criticize the affidavits of the people on the strength of which his application for a new trial was denied. He criticized them with sarcasm, on the ground that they were all metered and that their periods rhymed. With scorn he spoke of the procuring of a lot of affidavits from young schoolgirls to prove that Helen Potts was never addicted to the use of morphine, and of the procuring of a similar affidavit from a servant who could not read or write.

"Five hundred or a thousand years may pass away," said he, "and then you will hear some learned antiquarian discoursing before an assembled multitude. He has unearthed the records of the Court of General Sessions of the County of New York. He is explaining to the assembled crowd that at the close of the nineteenth century schoolgirls were so educated that they had reached the altitude of scientific knowledge when their expert observations were submitted to a learned court in a matter of life and death, and he might say that there was one witness, one lady, whose signature is a trifle obscure, who, although continuously a domestic in the family of George Potts, was able to tell at a glance the difference between powdered morphine and others, and, your Honor, Prof. Doremus told me last Sunday no expert can tell that without some test."

Taking up the affidavits which had been offered in support of his motion for a new trial, Harris said that the District Attorney had tried to make them all out perjuries. Doctor Traverton had been made to swear that his cook,

Mrs. Lewis, was of unsound mind because she had dared to make affidavit that Helen Potts had told her that she took morphine. Ethel Harris had been accused by a Philadelphia detective of having eloped when she could have been only thirteen years old because she had dared to make affidavit that Helen Potts had not only taken morphine but given it to her. Other witnesses who had made affidavits to the same effect, ladies of unquestioned reputation, had been bullied by Choate, who then made affidavits as to what they told him which they had repudiated. One of his witnesses had been declared unworthy of credence because she was once a member of the Salvation Army. . . .

Harris referred to the manner in which several of the jurors who had convicted him had stated that if the evidence which he offered in the affidavits on the motion for a new trial had been presented on the original trial they would have acquitted him. He had one more such affidavit, made by Crawford Mason yesterday, which he read, in which Mr. Mason said that he had known Dr. H. S. Kinmouth for eight years as an honest and upright man, and that if he, as a juror, had heard Dr. Kinmouth swear, as he has since sworn, that he used to sell morphine to Helen Potts, he would unhesitatingly have acquitted Harris.

Harris's strength seemed about to be exhausted at this time. The courtroom had been very still, and Recorder Smyth was sitting bolt upright looking straight into the eyes of the doomed young man. . . . There were tears in the eyes of many there as Harris turned to lawyer Howe, and in a trembling voice told him that for all he had done in his behalf he had inspired in his heart an affection that was only second to that he had for his mother. He handed to Mr. Howe an envelope, saying:

"I have not been able to recompense you. You know how poor I am. I ask you to accept this, though. It was the last gift of Helen to me, made the Christmas before she died."

The scene was a very touching one. The envelope contained a small pair of gold sleeve links. Mr. Howe burst into tears and leaned his gray head down upon his arms.

Harris finished very weakly after taking a long drink of the brandy and water. "I realize my position," he said. "No man could realize it better than I have realized mine day after day, and I know there is naught remains for me now but to meet my great misfortune with that fortitude which is the birthright of a gentleman and the prerogative of an innocent man."

. . .

There was a dry huskiness in the Recorder's voice as he began to speak. Harris interrupted him once to correct a statement. The Recorder said:

"My duty is made doubly painful in your case because you are undoubtedly a man of extraordinary intelligence, and I regret to see you standing in the position in which you do to-day. No one regrets it more sincerely than I do, and no one regrets more sincerely than I do that my sworn duty impels me to say that after listening to you with patience through all you have had to urge in your own behalf, I still adhere to what I stated upon your motion, that the evidence of your guilt was overwhelming in my view.

"In that statement and in that view I am upheld by seven judges of the Court of Appeals of this State, who, upon a fair review of all the testimony and upon the questions of law which were raised, unanimously came to the conclusion that the jury, upon the evidence which was then presented to them, could arrive at no other result than that to which they did arrive—that there were no errors of law committed by the Judge who tried the case by which your rights were in any way prejudiced by the court. And that learned court in closing their opinion stated that the law was accurately and properly laid down by the Judge.

"Now a motion came before me then upon evidence under a section of the code which requires me to state, in my opinion, the weight of the evidence which you had presented, and which if it had been presented to the jury, would have produced a different result. I could only examine that evidence with great care and with a conscientious desire to arrive at a proper and just conclusion.

"I, under the solemnity of my oath, and understanding a full sense of the obligation that I hold here and hereafter, am forced to the conclusion at which I arrived, that the evidence did not justify me in doing what I hoped to have done in a case of this magnitude."

Speaking then of his specific duty under the statute as to fixing the date for the execution of the sentence, the Recorder, in a scarcely audible voice, named the week beginning May 8, 1893.

Harris did not turn a hair when the final words were spoken. He was too far gone for that. He got on his feet, however, after a moment or two and said:

"I know that your Honor has not meant to do anything unjust. I know that according to the law it is all right; but the laws are changing every year. I believe that though this may be the last—that this is the last—of Carlyle Harris, this will also be the last of school-girl experts, and it also will be the last time that one fallible, honest magistrate is called upon to pass alone on life and death upon testimony sworn to by perjurers."

Then, gentleman, in manner at least, until the last, Harris stretched his hand over the railing toward the Recorder, made the motion as though shaking hands with him, and said with a polite bow:

"The issues of to-day aside, I beg the court to believe that the courtesy which has been shown to me will be in my mind, and gratefully so, to my dying day."[3]

Carlyle Harris was put to death on the Monday of the week specified. He died with a declaration of absolute innocence upon his lips. The execution was very impressive in the death chamber itself, in the house where Harris's mother was staying, and about the prison in general. More than a thousand people thronged into the little village and stood on the hill directly in front of the prison, waiting to see the little flag go up telling the world that Harris was no more.

He slept soundly for the last few hours that were allotted to him on this earth. Rising early, he started writing on a document which he wanted published after his demise. He ate breakfast, and after finishing up his writing, received Chaplain Wills for prayers and religious comfort.

He refused any stimulant and told Warden Durston that he wanted to make a brief statement just before he was placed in the chair. Shortly after noon, the chaplain returned again and more prayers were offered. The chaplain later declared that Harris seemed to have high ideas about life and death; that he was the most intelligent and sincere person that he had ever prepared for an execution.

Principal Keeper Connaughton escorted Harris into the death chamber.

> The condemned man was dressed in plain black, with no collar or necktie. The right leg of his trousers had been cut off at the knee, so that the electrode could be applied there, and the hair had been cut from the crown of the head for the same purpose.
>
> Harris walked alone. He stood erect. Chaplain Weills was just behind him, reading quietly the prayer of commendation from the Episcopal Prayer Book. The doomed man looked strange without his beard, which was shaved off when he was taken to the prison. His face was set and resolute. His eyes had the quizzical expression that was peculiar to them.
>
> He looked calmly at the witnesses and then at the chair. Without a tremor he walked to the chair, and just as he was sitting down said in a voice that was strong and unshaken:
>
> "I wish to say a word, and I think I have the Warden's permission to say it."

He motioned to the Warden gracefully as he spoke and bowed his head.

"What is it you wish to say?" asked Warden Durston.

"I have no further motive for any concealment whatever," answered the man whom life was to leave within a few seconds. Then he raised his head and ran his eyes along the line of witnesses' faces as he continued, "I desire to state that I die absolutely innocent of the crime of which I have been convicted."

That was all. He settled back in the chair and himself adjusted his limbs for the straps and electrodes. Everything ready, the handkerchief was dropped, and the current turned on. The body became rigid. In an instant the lips parted and the air in the lungs was discharged by the muscular contraction.

The current was kept on for four seconds at 1,760 volts. Then it was reduced at once to 150 volts and kept that way for 51-3/4 seconds. It was then turned off entirely. The doctors went to the chair, examined the body with instruments, and at 12:43 o'clock pronounced the man dead. He really died the instant the current was turned on.

. . .

When the little black flag was run up on the pole of the Warden's house announcing that the execution had taken place, Mrs. Harris and her son Allan could see it from the window of Ambler's boarding house, where they were stopping. Mrs. Harris did not weep. She had got past tears. Turning to Allan, she simply said:

"They have murdered him."[4]

Later that afternoon, she received newspaper men and started to talk to them in a most dramatic manner:

"They have murdered my son because he did not wail and gnash his teeth when he heard of his wife's death," said she. "But see how calm I am. Would they say I murdered my son because I do not carry on? I have not shed a tear.

I may not do so. Yet, do you not know that I loved my murdered boy dearly?

"My boy is free. He has gone where he will be taught and educated. You saw that he died like a brave man. He died protesting his innocence. Now he is safe. He was worldly and was somewhat immoral, but this thing brought him to a knowledge of his God.

"Who killed my boy? It was Tammany and the Potts family money and influence. Tammany killed him! Tammany killed him! I suppose the Potts family is satisfied now. What have they got out of it? My boy is dead, but their daughter has not been brought back. But it has all brought to me a clearer view of my God, and my children have been made Christians by it. So I may praise God for it all.

"Now I leave him in the hands of you newspaper men. Don't one of you dare to call him 'Murderer' Harris. Don't you dare to call him that. Call him the murdered Harris. Stand up for him. Did he not die bravely? Did he not die innocent?"

The woman was not talking hysterically, but slowly and earnestly.

"Did he not die innocent?" she again asked. There was no response save from one man, who said:

"He bore himself like an innocent man."

The silence seemed to anger the woman, and she cried again:

"Did he not die innocent? Shame on you all! Have the courage to break away from your nasty politics and answer with a hearty yes. You know he did. All right-minded men and women believed him innocent. That is why he died so bravely.

"The lesson to you young men, if there is a lesson, is that if you should ever be charged with a crime, and you should be innocent, run away. Carlyle did not run away, and he has been killed for a crime that he never committed. Now, good day."[5]

At 3 o'clock Undertaker Kipp drove up to the prison to get the body and prepare it for burial. He had a fine oak casket with a heavy silver plate, on which was inscribed:

CARLYLE W. HARRIS.
Murdered, May 8th, 1893.
Aged 23 years, 7 months, 15 days.
"We would not if we had known."
THE JURY.[6]

A Promise to Be Kept

From 1891 until 1898, there were twenty-five executions in the death house at Sing Sing. Carlyle Harris was the last person of note to meet his death until Mrs. Place was received for the murder of her stepdaughter. She was the first woman in the world to die by the electric current. Upon me fell the unpleasant duty of escorting her to the chair on March 20, 1899.

Though she was the first woman sent to the chair, Mrs. Place was the fifth to be executed in this state. Mrs. Margaret Houghteling was the first, being hanged at Hudson in 1817 six weeks after indictment for killing her child. She swore her innocence, and several years after, another woman confessed, on her deathbed, that she, not Mrs. Houghteling, had murdered the child. Mrs. Alice Runkle was next. She was hanged at the Whitesboro in 1849 after conviction for poisoning her husband. Mrs. Anne Hoag was also convicted for poisoning her husband. She was hanged at Poughkeepsie in 1852. Mrs. Roxalanna Druse was the last to die before Mrs. Place. She, too, killed her husband and was hanged in 1884.

On Monday morning, February 7, 1898, at her home, 598 Hancock Street, Brooklyn, Mrs. Place suffocated her stepdaughter, Ida, made a murderous assault on her husband with an axe, and then attempted to commit suicide. She confessed on the same day. Three complaints were lodged against her—one for murder, one for felonious assault, and a third for attempted suicide.

Mrs. Place had failed to kill herself, and after treatment at St. Mary's Hospital, was able to leave in the custody of the police who took her to the police station for questioning.

Mrs. Place was then taken to her home, where the police tried to obtain a confession from her for killing the stepdaughter. She resisted every effort made to have her see the remains, finally becoming so hysterical that she had to be led from the room. Back at police headquarters, she broke down and made a full confession.

"I struck my husband," she said slowly, dropping her head, "because I was afraid he was going to attack me. In the morning we had a violent quarrel, and I thought he would probably renew it. His daughter sided with him as she usually did, and slammed in my face the door of her room when I went to speak to her. That made me feel mad, so I got some acid from my husband's desk and threw it into her face. After that I didn't see her during the afternoon. I was fixing the furnace in the cellar when I saw the axe lying close by. It occurred to me that it would be very useful in case of trouble, so I took it up stairs with me. My husband came in afterward, and I struck him with it. That is all there is to it."

"Had you been drinking anything?" inquired the Police Captain.

"I had a few glasses of whisky and wine during the day, but nothing more. My husband always did find fault with me, anyhow. We were married six years ago. I had then been a widow six years, my first husband's name having been Wesley Lavcole.

"We had no children, but I had adopted a little boy, who is now fourteen years old. I took charge of him ten years ago, but my husband, while very attentive to his own daughter, would never permit my adopted boy to

live in the house with us. He is now in Orange, N. J.,
where I had him apprenticed to a harnessmaker. We were
married at my husband's home here in Brooklyn by the
Rev. Mr. Ostrander after having met a few months before
at Johnsonburg, N. J., my former home."[1]

Mr. Place, who was sent to the hospital with a compound frac-
ture of the skull, eventually recovered. He was in critical condition
for some time and the news of his daughter's death was kept from
him until he had been discharged from the doctor's care.

On July 12, Judge Hurd of the Kings County Court sentenced
Mrs. Place to die in the electric chair during the week of August
29th. The indifference shown by the woman throughout her trial
had entirely disappeared when she came up for sentence. In reply to
the usual questions of the court clerk, she was about forty-four years
old, married, lived in Brooklyn, was a Presbyterian, could read and
write, and had never before been convicted of any crime. She was
unable to reply when asked if she had anything to say on her own
behalf so her lawyer replied in the negative for her.

"Mrs. Place," said Judge Hurd, "the law fixes the
punishment you must endure for murder in the first degree.
The sentence of the court is that within ten days the
Sheriff of the county deliver you to the agent or Warden of
Sing Sing, and that sometime during the week beginning
Monday, Aug. 29, 1898, you be put to death in the mode
and manner prescribed by law."

The prisoner was sent at once by Sheriff Creamer to
the Grand Central Station. She was accompanied by the
jail matron, Fanny Handy; the city missionary, Miss Meury;
Warden Bergen, and Deputy Sheriff Wilson.[2]

Mrs. Place arrived at the prison on the day she was sentenced a
little over an hour after she had left the courtroom. She was brought
up the hill from the railroad station in a carriage. I happened to be in
the warden's office when she arrived, and she appeared to be deeply

affected as she entered the building. She held her handkerchief to her eyes and was weeping convulsively. Warden Sage met her at the door and escorted her into the clerk's office. She turned over some money and jewelry. Even her hairpins had to be removed. After the clerk had obtained the required information, she was taken to the old hospital building and placed in a room on the top floor. This room was formerly occupied by another murderess, Marie Barberi, but she was not executed. Mrs. Place let herself go when she entered the room and completely broke down. Efforts were made to console her, but they had little effect. She kissed the matrons goodbye and threw herself upon the bed exhausted. A matron was stationed in the room to watch over her constantly while a male guard stood just outside the door. Everything possible was done to make the woman comfortable, but she sobbed continually for the first few days of her confinement.

Due to many delays through appeals and other details, Mrs. Place was not put to death during the week specified. She remained in the old hospital from July 1898 until March of the following year. During the last few days of her confinement, I was assigned to do guard duty outside of her door. I was told to keep a close watch as the time for her execution was drawing near; the warden wanted to be sure that she did not kill herself and "beat the chair." She had tried suicide once. There was every reason to believe that she might make another attempt.

The first thing I found out was that Mrs. Place was allowed to walk up and down a stairway about twenty feet high. I locked that door immediately since she could have easily thrown herself down the steps in an attempt to end her life. She was greatly offended by what I had done and she said I was stopping her exercise. I told her I would take her out for all the exercise she wanted, but she was very angry with me. Finally, the day arrived when she was to die. Warden Sage called in the morning and told her to prepare for the last walk she would take on this earth. She seemed to have nerved herself for the ordeal and took this warning very coolly.

Condemned people are generally executed on the first day of the week during which they are to die. There have been cases when executions have been delayed until later, but after the first night, the doomed person is generally past the stage where he can go calmly to the chair.

There was quite some discussion as to whether Mrs. Place should be removed to a cell in the death house when her last day came or if she should remain in the hospital. Both places present equal difficulties. The woman might have received a great shock and been in a state of collapse if taken to a cell in the death house. Then, on the other hand, the long walk with so many turnings, ascents, and descents that she had to take on her last trip from the hospital might have prolonged the suspense. The warden finally decided to leave the woman where she was.

I didn't want Mrs. Place to be angry with me when she went to the chair so I talked to her. "Mrs. Place," I said, "I know you feel hard toward me, but I want to tell you something. Whenever the bell rang down there on that door, I couldn't get there quick enough because I knew it would be someone to see you who would cheer you. And when you lay down to rest, I stopped all work in the yard outside so you wouldn't be disturbed—so you could sleep away your time on earth without worrying. I tried to make it as easy as possible for you and I want you to know it."

"I'm sorry, Mr. Conyes," she said. "I know you have done everything you could for me. But there is just one thing more you can do. Promise me you will do it."

"I promise," I replied. "What is it you want me to do?"

"Put me in the chair," she declared.

Now, I had seen many men die in the chair, but the idea of strapping a woman into it was something different. However, I had promised and so I agreed to do as she wished, if the warden would give his permission. Mrs. Place spoke to him and he granted the request.

Mrs. Place went to her death calmly. Warden Sage read the sentence to her. Taking her arm, I escorted her down the steps, across the prison yard and into the death house. Behind us, walked the warden, two keepers, a woman physician, Mrs. Place's spiritual advisor, the Reverend Dr. Cole of Yonkers, and one of the prison matrons. The doomed woman was attired in a black gown which she had made to wear at an expected new trial. Having failed to get such a trial, she asked Governor Roosevelt to commute her sentence to life imprison-ment, but the petition was refused.

In one hand she held a small prayer book. Her eyes were closed, but she held her head erect. Her lips moved in prayer, and as she was seated, murmured, "God help me."

I quickly attached the electrodes after strapping in her feet. So great was the modesty in those days that a woman attendant spread her skirts before Mrs. Place so that the witnesses could not see her

FIGURE 25. The electric chair—at her request Alfred Conyes escorted Mrs. Place to the execution chamber and strapped her into the chair. Photo courtesy of Guy Cheli.

ankle as the electrodes were put into place against her calf. After strapping her arms down and tightening the broad belts across her chest, I stepped back and signaled the warden that all was ready.

The clergyman walked quietly away from the chair just before the current was turned on. The women attendants pressed close up against the chair. The body scarcely moved. The prayer book in the woman's left hand twisted across the wrist and slipped partly out as the muscles relaxed. Her thin lips simply tightened with the shock. The matron told me afterward that Mrs. Place had requested that the prayer book be given to me. I took it home and have it in my possession at the present time. Naturally, it is one of my most prized mementos.

FIGURE 26. A photo believed to be of a young Mrs. Place. Photo from the Conyes family archives.

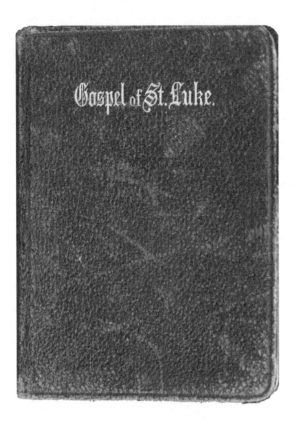

FIGURE 27. Mrs. Place's Gospel of Luke presented to Alfred Conyes after her execution, at her request. Photo from the Conyes family archives.

The current which had passed through the body of Mrs. Place had a power of about 1,760 volts and was kept on for four seconds. My opinion coincided with that of the others who had witnessed the execution—death was instantaneous. However, we always gave a second shock at Sing Sing and Mrs. Place was no exception. The body remained in the chair until all the witnesses had filed out of the room. Then an autopsy was held behind closed doors. The electrodes scarcely left a mark. The record of the autopsy, however, was kept a secret for some time after because of a question which had been raised as to Mrs. Place's sanity.

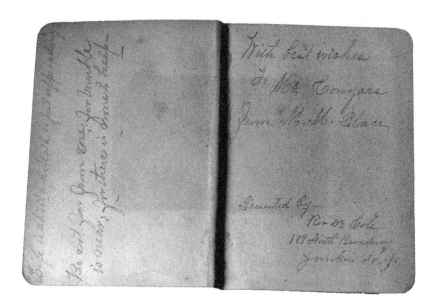

FIGURE 28. Inscription inside the Gospel of Luke written by Mrs. Place to Alfred Conyes. Photo from the Conyes family archives.

Governor Roosevelt showed great foresight when he requested that one or two women be admitted to the death chamber. They did their duty well. The woman physician was extremely capable and rapid in her movements. She knew her business.

Warden Sage was highly pleased with the result of the execution and sent a telegram to the state superintendent of prisons saying that the execution was entirely successful; that there were no revolting features; and that Mrs. Place met her death with fortitude.

The changed attitude of the press from the stand they had taken after the first few executions may be noted in the following editorial from the *New York Times*:

In the Central Federated Union on Sunday a motion was made to petition Gov. ROOSEVELT to commute the sentence of death for Mrs. PLACE to imprisonment for life, on the ground that the Union in its constitution opposed capital punishment. The motion was almost unanimously rejected. Its opponents took the ground that while they did not believe in capital punishment, they did believe in the full and impartial enforcement of the law. They wanted the law amended, not evaded. Especially they objected to an exception in the case of Mrs. PLACE on the ground that she was a woman. This strikes us as a peculiarly interesting and significant expression of public sentiment.

It is plain that the cause of the abolition of capital punishment has not received any special advantage from the execution yesterday. The incident in the Federal Union is entirely in line with the vote in the Assembly last week. Not only does not the execution of a woman under the same conditions as apply to men arouse particular feeling, but the general sentiment against the death penalty is certainly no stronger than it was a score of years ago. We very much doubt if it is as strong. People may have become less sensitive on the subject as population has increased, and individual crime attracts less attention than formerly, but whatever the cause, the old arguments seem to have lost their hold. . . .

It is to be noted also that the frantic efforts of the sensational press to arouse excitement over the execution of Mrs. PLACE have fallen very flat. So, we assume, will the fictitious accounts of the scene of execution. Gov. ROOSEVELT'S sensible and wise precautions made it certain that there could be no genuine pictures and no special descriptions. Of course this does not prevent the publication of descriptions that pretend to be special and of pictures taken at the very moment. We do not pretend to know how many people in New York enjoy even real photographs of a dying prisoner. But there cannot be a large number of this class—which we hope is not large—who care to be cheated by bogus pictures and invented details, helped out by cheap adjectives and cheaper moralities.[3]

The next prominent figure to be lodged in the death house was Albert T. Patrick. His case was, and still is, one of the most famous in the criminal annals of the United States. He was charged with the murder of William Marsh Rice, a Texas multimillionaire, which was committed on September 23, 1900. He was arrested on October 4 of the same year on a charge of forgery, but was not indicted for murder until the following May. Finally, after a long trial, he was found guilty on March 26, 1902, and sentenced to die on the 7th of the following month. Patrick put up a tremendous fight for his life, which ultimately resulted in a pardon from Governor Dix ten years after, in 1912.

His great struggle attracted general attention and convinced those who were familiar with the circumstances that, although he did not meet much success in his practice at the bar, he possessed a keen legal mind and was capable of doing good work in his profession.

A fortune was spent to save Patrick. His brother-in-law, John T. Milliken of St. Louis, spent over $500,000 on the defense. No one outside of Mr. Milliken's confidence was in a position to know just how much was actually paid, but the sum was certainly enormous and most people estimated it at approximately that figure. Some of the most talented lawyers in the country were procured by Milliken. Various experts were retained to consult about the questions involved in the trial. Detectives scoured the country and scores of witnesses were brought to New York and entertained in a lavish display of luxury.

Recorder John W. Goff pronounced the death sentence upon Patrick. Just as soon as the defendant had been arraigned for judgment, the District Attorney jumped to his feet, saying:

"If your Honor please, Albert T. Patrick was convicted of murder in the first degree at this term of the court and I now ask that judgment be pronounced." Patrick had come into court with a marked swagger. He stood with his arms behind him, one hand holding the other.

Clerk Carroll asked the prisoner if he had reason to give why judgment should not be pronounced. Mr. House, attorney for the defense, arose and read eight technical motions for a new trial.

Recorder Goff denied the motions and Mr. House said:

"We take an exception to your ruling and we move now for an arrest of judgment, first, because the facts stated in the indictment do not constitute a crime; second, because the indictment charges more than one crime in a single count; third, because it does not appear from the record of the verdict of what crime the defendant has been found guilty; and, fourth, because of errors apparent upon the face of the verdict.

This motion was denied and Mr. House said he had nothing further to offer.

Recorder Goff then, with softly modulated tones, read his judgment which was as follows:

"Albert T. Patrick, the judgment of the Court is that you, Albert T. Patrick, for the murder of the first degree of William Marsh Rice, whereof you are convicted, be, and hereby are, sentenced to the punishment of death; and it is ordered that, within ten days after this day's session of court, the Sheriff of the Country of New York deliver you together with the warrant of this court, to the agent and warden of the State Prison of the State of New York at Sing Sing where you will be kept in solitary confinement until the week beginning Monday, the 5th day of May, 1902; and upon someday within the week so appointed, the said agent and warden of the State Prison of the State of New York at Sing Sing is commanded to do execution upon you, Albert T. Patrick, in the mode and manner prescribed by the laws of the State of New York."

Patrick left at once for the Grand Central Station in his carriage accompanied by the sheriff. While sitting in the smoking car handcuffed to a Deputy Sheriff, Patrick drew up a legal document which he served on Warden Johnson at Sing Sing Prison and also on Sheriff William J. O'Brien in which he served notice of appeal and protested against any execution or partial execution of the judgment and against the delivery of his person by Sheriff O'Brien to Warden Johnson. In explanation of this proceeding, Patrick said that it was his interpretation of the law that the weeks spent in solitary confinement were a part of the punishment and that the law never contemplated that, while the prisoner's case was on appeal, he should be kept in solitary confinement.[4]

Patrick spent nearly five years in the death house, and after being sentenced to death seven times, he was saved from the chair by Governor Higgins. The death sentence was commuted to life imprisonment on December 20, 1906.

Patrick was extremely gratified that his life was to be spared, but he declared that his efforts to obtain a complete freedom and vindication would be continued. He said that he would fight through all the courts and would never rest until the United States Supreme Court had passed upon his case.

Friends of the prisoner insisted that the acceptance of the commutation was merely a temporary expedient to give them time to take further steps for his release. Patrick was bitterly opposed at the outset to the application to have his sentence commuted. If he could not be completely exonerated from the crime, he insisted that he preferred the death penalty.

When the governor intimated that he would consider a request for a commutation of the sentence and make Patrick a present of his life for Christmas, all the relatives of the condemned man united in urging him to accept the gift. They assured the imprisoned man that there would be no cessation in their struggle in his behalf. After all kinds of persuasion, Patrick finally gave his consent.

There was some delay in the arrival of the commutation papers, but a few days later Patrick was released from the death house and led to the clerk's office, where he was subjected to the same treatment that all newcomers received.

After he had been measured and weighed, he was clad in a suit of gray prison clothes with four bars on the left sleeve of his coat, one for each year he had served. Warden Johnson told me to conduct the prisoner to the door and sash factory.

When Patrick appeared in the workshop where he was to start work, he at once became the center of attraction. Although the convicts were forbidden to glance about on any occasion, none were able to resist stealing a glance at him. Under the circumstances, I allowed this infraction of the rules to pass unnoticed.

Patrick expressed great interest in the duties of the men and listened attentively while I explained the work in detail. I saw him later in the day still intent on grasping this new phase of prison life. As the men filed by him, I suggested that he fall in line and he quickly complied, evidently enjoying the new sensation.

On the way to the cells, the men received a piece of ginger bread and a dipper full of tea—the usual supper fare. Patrick carried his to his cell, which was number 1074 in Gallery 22. I introduced him to his new keeper and left him sitting on the side of his bunk sampling his first taste of the regular prison fare.

Men in the death house are allowed privileges forbidden in the regular prison routine. Patrick told me that he was afraid he would have a hard time in the new atmosphere. His cell in the death house had been a roomy one; he could read all the books and magazines he wished, and visitors were allowed to come to see him often. There was no doubt that Patrick had the keenest mind of any who had ever been confined in the death house.

As a life convict, he was now obliged to spend his free time in the narrow regulation cell; he could have only an occasional book, and visitors were allowed to see him only at certain intervals. The food was, of course, vastly different, consisting, at the time, of bread and coffee for breakfast, soup and meat or fish for dinner, and ginger bread and tea for supper.

He worked steadily and well in the door and sash factory until the time of his pardon on November 28, 1912, Thanksgiving Day. Governor Dix decided that the Court of Appeals was sufficiently doubtful to warrant his granting a pardon to Patrick. Once again, a tumult arose, the newspapers joining in with sensational articles and statements for and against the governor's action.

Governor Dix will undoubtedly go out of office with a fine record of amiability. The pardoning of Albert T. Patrick, of whose guilt there has been very little doubt in the minds of the public or in the minds of those intimately connected with his case, has attracted so much attention that sight is likely to be lost of the numerous other pardons that the Governor has granted, and yet the news comes from Albany that he has two hundred more cases which he expects to dispose of before the end of his term.

The pardoning power is the official prerogative of the Governor which none may limit although many may criticize. The pardoning of a burglar convicted of a second offense in 1909 and sentenced for life undoubtedly will be challenged by many who are prone to think that one who has been convicted of burglary twice is not likely to be reformed.

But—

"The quality of mercy is not strained and earthly power doth more than show likest God's when mercy seasons justice." And, furthermore, the Governor is the judge and the jury is his own conscience.[5]

A Narrow Escape, Suicide, and Tragedy

Throughout all these executions, I continued working in the stone shed. There had been a shortage of men who understood blasting due to the release of several inmates who had served out their terms. The keeper in charge of the quarries asked me if I had anyone who might be able to help him out. Lester Phibbs offered to assist, and I sent him over.

He had not been in the quarries very long before he started fighting with one of my men who was employed in bringing stone from there to the cutting shed. They were continually pecking at each other and often came to blows, so I had to separate them by keeping my man in the shed.

Phibbs apparently had received the worst of their many encounters. He wanted to settle accounts between them once and for all. Many plans began to formulate in his mind until he decided that the best way to settle the differences was to blow the other fellow to bits.

It was easy for Phibbs to carry off an odd stick of dynamite. He put one into his blouse and walked casually into the stone shed taking care that no one should notice him. The object of his wrath was working on a pile of flagging which had been heaped up near my desk. Carefully removing several of the larger pieces, Phibbs hid the explosive at the bottom of the pile in the hope that my assistant would strike it with his sledge hammer.

Several days passed and nothing happened. Then an inmate, Keeler, by name, came up to me and said, "Mr. Conyes, I know it's not so good for convicts to tell on one another, but you've been mighty nice to me and I haven't the least desire to see you spattered all over the landscape. If you'll look in that pile of stone there by your desk, you mind find something well worth getting rid of."

I removed the stone, and sure enough, there was the charge with the cartridges all ready to go off at the bottom of the pile. In spite of Phibbs's precautions, he must have been seen by Keeler. I made some investigations of my own and discovered that Phibbs was the man responsible. I said very little about it, simply suggesting to the principal keeper that he take Phibbs from the quarry and put him to work removing rubbish with a wheelbarrow. This was done that very afternoon, and Phibbs was always kept far out of reach of any high explosives.

Immediately after this event, one of the most uncanny suicides in the history of the prison took place when John McDermott took his life. He had served seven years of a life term for killing his wife. McDermott had often threatened suicide, but was carefully watched. However, his chance finally came. While at work in the mess hall, he stuck his head and shoulders into the furnace, burning himself to death.

A similar incident occurred when I was in charge of the foundry. Benny Braxton was one of the most forlorn figures in the prison. I tried to make him work, but he always whined and refused to do anything. I often had to punish him, but the punishment had little effect. One day, he came to me and said, "You're not going to work me anymore, Mr. Conyes. You're not going to punish me either. I've had enough of this and I'm going to put a stop to it."

Before I could stop him, he had walked over to the fire in the forge and burned his eyes out by holding his face over it. Naturally, he passed out, but a few days later, when he was feeling better, he came into the shop and smiled at me, apparently very happy in spite of the loss of his eyesight.

"Mr. Conyes," he said, "I told you, you weren't going to work me anymore, and now you won't be able to punish me either."

He died about six months later and was buried in the prison cemetery. I don't believe he had a friend in the world. He was probably better off in the grave.

I doubt very much if Sing Sing ever had a more audacious swindler than George Williams, who sometimes passed as George Hart. He was a remarkably clever forger. While at the prison, Williams was a "trusty" in the warden's residence. When he was released, he managed to take a large quantity of the warden's printed stationery along with him.

Forging the signature, he wrote letters on this paper to prosperous friends of the prison head asking them to lend the bearer, Williams, money. He made a living in this manner for over five months until he was apprehended in Brooklyn. Arraigned before Police Justice McNeal in the Village of Ossining, he was charged with swindling Principal Keeper John Derenbecker and held for the Grand Jury.

Just a short time before, a sensation occurred in the death house. Carl Fiegenbaum, a murderer, told his keepers that a ghost had entered his cell through the bars of his door in an attempt to kill him. William Caesar, another slayer, had died suddenly in the same cell only a week before. Fiegenbaum leaped from his cot screaming at the top of his voice and calling for help. His body was covered with a cold sweat and his eyes were staring out of their sockets. He said he had seen an apparition of Caesar, which had seized and throttled him. Efforts were made to calm the terrified murderer, but he finally had to be transferred to another condemned cell before he became normal. Fiegenbaum had been sentenced to die for choking his wife to death, and that led most of us to believe it the cause of his scare.

I also had a part in the search which was conducted for James Keenan, who made a sensational attempt to escape, even though it was unsuccessful. We missed him from the supper count on May 28, 1896. It seems while working as a mason on a prison building, he had walled off a secured compartment just large enough to hide himself in. After his disappearance, he would stay in this hiding place throughout the day, always on watch for a chance to get through the gates or over the wall. At night, he would remove the loose bricks, come out and raid the larder of John Y. McKane, the wealthy Coney Island politician. McKane always had plenty of delicacies on hand, and Keenan managed to get away with enough food to allow him to subsist while hiding.

We knew we would have little opportunity to discover him during the daytime. Consequently, the search was conducted at night for nearly two weeks before we discovered that he was stealing from McKane's refrigerator. Then we knew he was still somewhere within the walls, but the problem was to find his hiding place. The following night, we called the guards out of the enclosure and waited just outside. Keenan took the bait. He thought our search was off and decided to make his dash for freedom. Just as he was coming around the end of one of the walls, he ran head-on into us and was retaken with very little trouble.

The politician John Y. McKane came to Sing Sing in 1894 after being convicted of violating voting laws. The first night he was in the prison he begged me for a drink. I told a "trusty" to get him some water and bring it to his cell. When he had served his time and was leaving the prison, he thanked me and said: "I would have been willing to give $500 for that drink of water that night, Mr. Conyes. I was ill and needed it badly."

There were several famous swindlers in Sing Sing at this time also. Francis Weeks, a disbarred lawyer, got away with over a million dollars by robbing estates. He served his time and left the prison in a private railroad car, which took him somewhere out west. He still had that money. "Al" Adams was always lounging around the hospital ward. He never seemed to do anything but sit. He made something like ten million dollars in a get-rich-quick scheme.

On Sundays, when the shops were closed, I often put in extra time doing guard duty in the cell block or death house. One day, a prisoner called to me and told me that the inmate in the cell next to him was having fits. He didn't look so bad to me, but I took him to the hospital anyway. I told the doctor my suspicions, and after a thorough examination, the man was pronounced perfectly healthy without a sign of any trouble. Instead of being confined to a bed in the hospital as he had hoped, the inmate was thrown into the dungeon for several days until he recovered from his "illness." He told me later that he and the fellow next to him took turns in feigning illness so that they might take things easy in the hospital ward for a few days at a time. They never went to that place again unless they really had to be taken there.

Then, while I was on duty in the death house, an inmate refused to give up his dishes when I went around collecting them after the evening meal.

"If you want my dishes, let's see you come in and get them," he threatened.

"All right," I replied, "I'm on my way."

There was a bit of a scuffle and the interior of the cell didn't look so good when it had subsided, but I had the dishes and that particular person never gave out any more threats.

On February 28, 1908, Captain William H. Van Schaick, who claimed to be the victim of the saddest marine disaster in the history of the state, stumbled into Sing Sing Prison. He was to serve a sentence for criminal negligence in failing to observe the navigation law while in command of the steamboat General Slocum on June 15, 1904.

The case is somewhat similar to the later Vestris catastrophe. The General Slocum was burned to the water's edge in the East River off Northern Brother Island with a loss of 1,030 lives. The boat had been chartered for an excursion by St. Mark's German Lutheran Church of 323 East Sixth Street. Nearly all the dead were women and children.

The party of 1,400 people left the East Third Street dock at 9:30 on the morning of June 15, 1904. The boat started upstream, passing through Hell Gate while children ran happily all over the ship and mothers gathered on the upper deck to enjoy the sunshine.

The vessel was opposite 130th Street before the fire was noticed. Some people thought they saw smoke before then, but believed it to be coming from the chowder which was being cooked on the lower deck. The dread warning sounded through the boat about one hour after it had left the pier. No sooner had the people become aware of the impending disaster than there was a tremendous explosion followed by a huge sheet of flame which enveloped the forward part of the boat. Within a few moments, the flames had driven the passengers far back into the stern. Then pandemonium broke loose on board. The frilly holiday dresses of the women and children quickly caught fire and many died before they could get to the life boats. Women were roasted to death within sight of their husband and children. Babes by the score perished in the waters of the East River where they had been thrown by frenzied mothers. There was no alternative. With death by fire behind them, hundreds leaped into the river only to perish before help could reach them. Watermen, policemen, nurses and physicians saved hundreds at the risk of their own lives.

Instead of turning the vessel to the New York shore close at hand, Captain Van Schaick carried it to North Brother Island and ran it on the rocky shore. He explained this by saying that he had been warned off because of fear the great lumber yards on the New York shore might catch fire.

The crew made no attempt to get order out of the frightful panic. Life preservers rotted away in the hands of those who tried to use them as many contained sawdust instead of the usual cork material. A few members of the crew managed to bring a hose into play, but the pumps wouldn't work, and it was snatched from their hands by the frenzied women.

Captain Van Schaick stuck to his post until the pilot house caught fire. The boat was then about twenty-five yards off North Brother Island. Many more people jumped into the water at this point, and the captain followed them, wading ashore. There had been little chance to lower the lifeboats, and those that were lowered sank at once.

The captain was immediately taken to the police station, where he was questioned by the officials and held on a charge of neglect in failing to hold lifeboat drills and inspect the hose and life preservers. He was tried and convicted in the United States District Court before Judge Thomas, receiving a sentence of ten years imprisonment at hard labor.

He arrived at Sing Sing on February 27, 1908. That morning, addressing reporters at the Federal Building in New York, he concluded a statement with these remarks:

"The prosecution at my trial laid great stress on the fact that I did not hold regular fire drills, as described in the Federal regulations. How could I? The *Slocum* had only been in commission a few days at that time, and drills are only possible when a boat is steadily in commission and has a regular crew. I had only what is called a scrub crew, one of the members of which was on the boat but three days, and another but five days. It is all very well to talk of proper equipment, but to put a vessel in first-class trim costs a lot of money, and the chances are that, if I had ordered all the things the *Slocum* required, I would have been out of a job. I hope for a pardon. I am not in America if I don't get it. I am the victim of circumstances."[1]

Van Schaick's record had been a good one. Since the day of her launching, he had been in command of the *General Slocum* and was credited with being one of the best pilots about New York. He knew every foot of the ground around the harbor. Although he had been in a number of accidents, he suffered more from bad luck than from ignorance. He was sixty-one years of age at the time of the disaster. His home, since 1891, had always been just aft of the pilot house on the hurricane deck of the vessel during sailing seasons. His employers regarded him as a most capable, careful, and reliant man who was always ready to protect their interests and those of his passengers at any cost.

Between his conviction and his trip to the prison, he married Grace Mary Spratt. She was superintendent of the Lebanon Hospital in the Bronx at the time of the disaster and led a party of eight nurses in caring for the survivors. Mrs. Van Schaick was many years his junior, and for fourteen years had refused to marry him, but when life was darkest for the old man, she married him a few days before he left for Sing Sing.

I saw the captain when he was admitted to the prison—a broken, feeble, old man. He leaned against the office railing while being questioned by the prison clerk. Tears were trickling down his cheeks and he had to be assisted whenever he took a step. I took him into the barber shop where his mustache was shaved off and his hair cut. His clothing was taken from him in the tailor shop, and after the customary bath, he received the prison suit which he put on at once. Then I took him to a cell in the old cell block. He threw himself on the bunk and his body was shaken by great sobs as he broke down completely after the long and trying ordeals through which he had passed. I felt very sorry for the old gentleman—more so than I have ever felt for anyone in the prison. Closing the cell door, I walked softly down the corridor, leaving him alone with nothing but the walls for company.

The following morning, Van Schaick was examined by Doctor Irvine to ascertain what kind of labor he was capable of doing. He appeared to be in fairly good health; his run-down condition due mostly to nervousness. However, out of respect to his old age, he was given a job in the greenhouse, where he performed light tasks. He soon became acclimated and took up his work cheerfully, always looking ahead to the pardon which he felt sure was coming.

The captain's wife had received a scroll in recognition of her great service in the rescue work at the tragedy, but it meant little to her when she saw the barred doors close behind the figure of her husband. She stood weeping at the prison door. Her husband might have been in disgrace in the eyes of the law, but he was a hero in her own. The disaster which brought about their marriage had also separated them almost immediately after. She set to work at once exerting every possible effort to get the captain out. She circulated petitions for his pardon, and after he had served two and a half years in prison, she got the pardon from President Taft on Christmas Day, 1912. I was in sympathy with the captain, and nobody was more pleased than I when we heard of his good fortune.

The pardons of Patrick and Van Schaick created such a furor, I think it advisable to go a bit into detail about the pardon system.

The law of the state makes the governor the source of pardons for prisoners in the state prisons. At the same time, the Prison Law provides elaborate rules for commutation. In each state prison there is a local board consisting of the warden, P. K., the physician and the superintendent of industries.

The board of the prison meets once a month and sends its recommendations to the governor. It also has full power to recommend the withholding of a commutation as a punishment for offenses against the prison discipline.

The proper or improper release of a prisoner depends upon the degrees of thoroughness and conscientious care with which this board makes its recommendations. There are thousands of items in each of their reports, and it is impossible for the governor to personally check them all. Still, he is held responsible if anything goes wrong. This places him in a poor position—one which he should never be in. At times, he is involved indirectly in the various pressures which are exerted to get prisoners out. At times—many, many times—the prisoner with the most backing is the least deserving.

The State Parole Board consists of three members—the state superintendent of prisons and two other appointed by the governor. It was originally established with jurisdiction over all first-offender criminals. Now, their power has been extended to definite-sentence prisoners after their release. Parts of this custody are delegated to various protectory societies and the Prison Association. This manner deals well enough with the first offenders, but the others should be left to the police.

The board meets monthly at the various state prisons. The three members and a clerk travel approximately 3,700 miles a month making a heavy state expense. Then, too, the two appointed members have to give up a great deal of their time—something they are not supposed to do. Consequently, they occasionally accept reports passed on to them without digging any too deeply into the facts. They are not experts well versed in criminology, and are more apt to be inclined toward the human side of the question. The benefit of the doubt is generally given to the prisoner rather than the community.

The governor should be freed of a load that is both unreasonable and unfair. A board of experienced judges would be able to deal more fairly with parole and pardon problems. The Prison Law should be changed so as to establish a contrast between the first offenders and the inveterate criminals. The prisoner's record should always be available, and the prison board should send in its recommendations free from any favoritism or "drag."

After Van Schaick's release, the couple purchased the George Stewart farm near Amsterdam, New York, with money raised by their friends, but within a year after moving there, they separated. The captain lived in seclusion for a number of years, finally moving to the Masonic Home in Utica, where he died on December 7, 1927, at the age of eighty-four.

Shortly after Captain Van Schaick arrived at the prison, I found myself transferred from the stone shed to the state (tailor) shop by the doctor's order. Just before leaving the place where I had been working for over twelve years, I met a man who had been sent up from Kingston, my old home town. As soon as he found out what my name was, he asked me if I was any relation to Jake Conyes of Plattekill. I told him I was as closely related to the man as I could be for he was my father.

"Well, now," said the prisoner, "what do you think of that, Captain? Jake Conyes served on the jury that convicted me and here I find you, his son, working me in this place. The world surely is pretty small at that, isn't it?"

After he had served his time, he went back to his home up the river. About a month after he had left, he sent me the Lord's Prayer, engraved by hand and beautifully framed.

Then there was a fellow whom I shall call George. He was my waiter and used to bring my lunch to me while I was in the shops. He had been in the prison for a little over nineteen years. Once in a while, I would leave a small piece of pie or something in the basket for him. Handing out any food to the men was against regulations, but he knew enough to eat what I had left for him. Later, when I was transferred, George came up to thank me.

"I want to thank you, sir," he said. "I've been in this place for almost twenty years and that pie you used to leave in the basket for me was the first I had had in all that time. It may seem a small thing, Mr. Conyes, but it tasted better than anything I have ever eaten. I certainly appreciate your kindness, and I wanted to tell you so before you left us."

A few months later I was marching a company of eighty into their cells for their evening meal. They were allowed four pieces of bread each from the "rack." I noticed George in the detail, and he seemed to be anxious about something.

"Halt!" I commanded. "George, what's the matter with you?"

"Well, Captain," he replied, "I'm a large man and I need all the food I can get in this place. It's hard enough to get along on what we do, but tonight, one of the keepers took a piece of my bread. I only have three slices now and I need that extra piece."

I looked down the line and asked the men if there were any who had more than they wanted. Five of them held up their hands. I took a slice from each and, walking back to George, I put them in his hand.

"There you are, George," I said. "That ought to hold you for a while. Now, let's not have any more complaining."

A few years later he went home. He never forgot the incident for I received a letter from him reminding me of it. I still hear from him occasionally. He tells me that he is working in New York and getting along very well. I never expect to see him again, but if I do, I hope it is not in Sing Sing.

Do Good and Make Good

·◆——————◆·

During the year 1914, the inmates of the two state prisons at Auburn and Sing Sing were given a large measure of self-government with the establishment of the Mutual Welfare League at Auburn and the Golden Rule Brotherhood at Sing Sing.

The organization at Sing Sing was established shortly after the appointment of Thomas Mott Osborne as warden. Sing Sing had four wardens during that year. The resignation of Warden James M. Clancy in June was followed by the appointment of Thomas J. McCormick. McCormick was removed from office because it was determined that he had shown favoritism to David Sullivan, who was serving time for his part in the wrecking of the Union Bank in Brooklyn, where he had been bank president. McCormick had made the prisoner his personal chauffeur and when accompanying him on outings in Yonkers and New York had left Sullivan on his own, unattended, multiple times. George S. Weed, chief clerk in the office of the superintendent of state prisons, served as acting warden until the appointment of Mr. Osborne.

During the following year, the Brotherhood also became known as the Mutual Welfare League. The League's primary purpose was to generate self-motivation in the prisoners. Members of the League were granted many substantial privileges by the warden. The prisoners were permitted to elect delegates to represent them. The number of these delegates was based on a unit of thirty men as distributed in the various shops and industries. They elected an executive committee of nine members, a secretary, and a treasurer, and enacted rules and regulations for the conduct of the society. This executive committee appointed a judiciary board of five members, various committees of the League, and the sergeant at arms.

Osborne's action was regarded as the most radical experiment in prison reform ever attempted. The unusual privileges he granted the prisoners caused comments from all sides. Interest in his methods was countywide, and both praise and criticism were offered through the columns of the newspapers. The State Prison Commission visited Sing Sing to investigate the conditions, and in its report, stated:

> Whatever may be the individual viewpoint toward prison discipline, every fair-minded citizen who investigates conditions in Sing Sing must admit that an extraordinary experiment is going on. So far as it has gone, while there may be many special conditions open to criticism which should be corrected and while mistakes may have been made, which is not surprising in so difficult an undertaking, the main results and achievements are constructive and progressive.[1]

Then, the commission recommended that the Osborne plan be fairly tried over a sufficient period of time to demonstrate its success or failure.

However, in September, the superintendent of prisons requested the district attorney of Westchester County to investigate fifteen cases of felonious assault that were believed to have taken place during the first six months of the year. The investigation proceeded with a special Grand Jury in October resulting in indictments against several inmates followed by one against Warden Osborne himself. George W. Kirchwey was named as his successor on December 31, 1915. Osborne, however, was reinstated as warden at Sing Sing on July 16, 1916.

The activities of the Mutual Welfare League have branched out since the arrival of Warden Lawes, who came to us on January 1, 1920. Lewis Lawes had served overseas in the World War and was superintendent of the New York City Reformatory for male misdemeanants at New Hampton Farms before his transfer to Sing Sing. He succeeded Daniel J. Grant, who had been placed in temporary charge of the prison after the resignation of Edward V. Brophy. Conditions at Sing Sing at the present time are the best possible. Warden Lawes has always been an enthusiastic supporter of the Mutual Welfare League and has carried on the splendid work. He seems to have a knack of judging a prisoner on an unbiased basis. A prisoner is not a prisoner with the warden. He is a human being who has done wrong and must be punished—not an animal for the guards to swing their clubs at. In my opinion, Warden Lawes has proved himself to be the finest of all the wardens at Sing Sing.

The Welfare League sergeant-at-arms preserves discipline and order in the various companies. Accordingly, each election group has a delegate and a sergeant-at-arms to represent them. These men are responsible for the behavior and conduct of the men in their units. Additional Welfare League officers are appointed when necessary.

The judiciary committee largely exercises the punishment in the institution. It hears complaints against the prisoners which are referred by both prisoners and prison officials alike. When charges are filed with the board, the accused men are summoned before the board and tried. If guilty, they are suspended from membership in the League. This suspension means confinement during recreation periods, loss of privileges, and a restriction on purchases from the commissary for a certain definite period. In all cases, an appeal may be taken to the Warden's Court, which is composed of the warden, the principal keeper, and the prison doctor. League privileges are highly prized by the prisoners, and it is a severe punishment to be deprived of them.

Ball games, tennis matches, and other athletic sports, moving picture shows, vaudeville, lectures, radio, and other entertainments are provided for the recreation of the prisoners. All equipment and incidental expenses are paid by members of the League through the

FIGURE 29. Baseball teams from each prison shop played intramural games inside the prison walls at Lawes Field. Photo courtesy of Guy Cheli.

League treasury. The store is stocked with provisions, cigarettes, candy, etc., which the inmates are permitted to trade.

Before the Mutual Welfare League, there was an armed guard in every shop. With clubs, they stood over the prisoners in the mess hall during meals and were everywhere about the place impressing their power on the inmates. Now, instead of remaining in the shops all the time, the guards regularly patrol them. Guards have been withdrawn from the mess hall, leaving most of the control to the officers of the League.

Many people still contend that the diminished authority of the guards is dangerous, but this is not so. All the machinery of the old system still remains in place. Warden Lawes reserves full power to

FIGURE 30. Warden Lawes pictured with the Mutual Welfare League's first-place baseball team, the Black Sheep. Photo courtesy of Michael DeVall.

veto the judgments of the prison judiciary board at any time, and occasionally he does so. Now, when walking about the prison, the casual visitor can see very few guards, but the prisoner knows he is being watched. He also knows that the guards are ready to respond to any emergency.

This system naturally allows the inmate a great deal more freedom. Some take advantage of the privilege and manage to make their escape, but modern police methods are fairly efficient, and it is not long before the culprit finds himself back where he started.

The following is the letter which is received by each new prisoner from the Mutual Welfare League when he is admitted to the prison:

As fellow inmates and members with you in the Mutual Welfare League, we wish to help make your lot here as tolerable as possible and we want your cooperation.

The warden, guards and other state officials here are charged with the duty of enforcing the State laws and prison rules. They hold their places only so long as they perform their duty. To maintain order and discipline at all times and require every person to perform a full day's efficient work—these are their primary duties.

Guards are on view and on duty everywhere at all times, and in an emergency, they will rigidly enforce the laws and rules, but you will soon learn that, acting under the Warden's instructions, they are all patient and considerate.

It is on the members of the Mutual Welfare League; it is on us—on your and our good sense—that the prison officials here rely for the observance and enforcement of laws and rules. Your and our privileges as members of the League, even your and our health, both of mind and body, are dependent upon you and our loyal observance of the laws and rules.

To say the Mutual Welfare League is wrong is an absurd statement. Anyone who has seen the prison conditions knows that the men must have this means of "doing something." It is a dangerous thing, of course, if it is not kept under control, but Warden Lawes is honest and just. The men all like him, and while he does allow them the usual privileges, they are given to understand that his word is final.

Warden's Court is held once a week, and all inmates who have broken any rules are brought before the court. These men are divided into different classes—A, B, and C. Class "A" men may have five visits a month and may spend three dollars each week in the commissary for groceries. This does not include cigarettes or other miscellaneous articles, however. Grade "B" men have only two visits a month. They are allowed to spend $1.50 a week for groceries. Grade "C" inmates have no visits without special permission from the warden. They must also have his permission to make any purchases in the commissary. In addition, the men have various periods of time added to their term in place of the old flogging method.

The work of the League at the present time may best be ascertained from its annual report, which is submitted to the warden in June of each year. The following is for the year ending June 30, 1929, and shows the good work done by the inmates themselves with their own funds.

TO THE HONORABLE
LEWIS E. LAWES,
WARDEN—INSTITUTION

Dear Sir:

I have the honor to submit, for your perusal and subsequent comment, the annual report of the Mutual Welfare League for the fiscal year, ending June 30, 1929.

It must be a source of profound satisfaction to the official staff at Sing Sing to know that the idea of self-government amongst inmates has proven a remarkable and efficacious instrument for pacifism and harmony in an institution whose very existence depends upon such a condition, and incidentally, is so essential to our welfare; and having emerged fundamentally intact from a year of perplexing and trying organization problems, we feel that the League has established itself upon a more solid foundation than ever before.

The transitory problem occupied the major portion of institutional activity and we feel safe in the assertion that the cooperation of every inmate lessened the possibility of any undue disorder. Indeed, nothing since the inception of the League parallels this phenomenal expansion and is significant of what will exist during the next six months, at least.

From the most cursory survey, the body of delegates which to date number fifty-four, have instilled in the hearts

of each inmate of their constituency the need for cooperation on their part. The League is fortunate in numbering
amongst their hundreds, delegates such as the incumbents
who have accomplished all that can be expected when
the occasion arose.

The sergeant-at-arms and his corps of twenty-two
deputies have done valid work in the administration of
their duties which are manifold, and with the exception
of one or two misunderstandings, they have proven of
valuable assistance to the League and to the official staff
of the prison.

Recreational activities have proven a real source
of harmony to our population and should be encouraged
as baseball, moving pictures, etc. are factors that will
banish depression and ill feeling, conditions that should
never exist amongst a population of our nature. Pessimists
would have us believe that toleration of sports, etc. within
prison walls is indicative of "coddling." They insist that
we should be placed in solitary cells and allow the key to
disappear because of some unfavorable incident that may
have occurred in the distant past. It is nonsense to pick
out isolated happenings and say that they represent the
progress of the whole scheme of things; for the Mutual
Welfare League has been a source of better understanding amongst men who are confined. Antiquated methods
of prison administration have been obscured by modern
penologists who unanimously agree that the "old system"
was totally inefficacious.

The officials can do just so much toward amelioration
of institutional conditions; after that, they are powerless and
their actions are governed by the actions of the inmates.
We all realize the importance of individual effort, for upon
it, all good or bad things depend. We can say, without fear
of contradiction, that the inmate population of our prison
today are firmly convinced that strict obedience to the
principles of the League and adherence to the institutional

rules and regulations is of vital importance to their welfare and every one of us should realize that disobedience and indifference can only result to our disadvantage.

Viewing the future outlook in all its broader aspects, there seems ample reason to hope for and to expect that the Mutual Welfare League will be of considerable assistance to the administration by acclimating inmates to our environment and to vernacularize "showing 'em the ropes." Encouragement from the officers and administration would be highly considered and welcome indeed and I am sure that the inmate population in general would appreciate their interest. Rehabilitation of the men confined is the all-important factor, and if the Mutual Welfare League can help one of its members towards an exemplary life, we shall feel that we have accomplished everything.

I quote from your speech to the American Prison Congress at Boston in 1923—in which you discuss the League thusly: "In Sing Sing Prison, there is a well-defined example of inmate organization and I have closely watched its effect for nearly four years, with much satisfaction as to results . . . The Mutual Welfare League helps to cultivate the needed sense of group responsibility; it creates a spirit of community interest instead of the old, narrow self interest . . . and I defy any man to say that this spirit of group responsibility cannot be cultivated within prison walls . . ."

In conclusion, the Mutual Welfare League takes this means to thank you, Warden, and the whole official staff for their diligent interest in our activities and you may be assured that the whole inmate population who revere and respect you and your methods, are always anxious and willing to assist towards the maintenance of our motto, "DO GOOD AND MAKE GOOD."

Very truly yours,
MUTUAL WELFARE LEAGUE
Frank Farrara
Secretary

FIGURE 31. Mutual Welfare League currency. Photo courtesy of Guy Cheli.

FINANCIAL STATEMENT

TOTAL ASSETS FOR THE TWELVE MONTH PERIOD:

FROM COMMISSARY	$7,200.00
PROCEEDS—ANNUAL SHOW—(1928)	2,254.00
BASEBALL COLLECTIONS AND DONATIONS	600.00
TOTAL ASSETS	$10,054.00

EXPENDITURES FOR THE TWELVE MONTH PERIOD:

LABOR DAY EVENTS	500.00
MOTION PICTURES	2,400.00
TRANSPORTATION (VAUDEVILLE)	500.00
FOURTH OF JULY—ICE CREAM, ETC.	400.00
COMMISSARY PURCHASES	1,000.00
FINANCIAL ASSISTANCE TO FAMILIES OF INMATES FOR RAILROAD TICKETS	817.00
FINANCIAL ASSISTANCE TO INMATES ABOUT TO BE RELEASED	1,000.00
INSTALLATION OF RADIO AMPLIFIERS	307.00
RADIO EARPHONES	300.00
UPKEEP OF RADIO	30.00

BASEBALL MATERIAL FOR LEAGUE TEAM AND
ENTIRE POPULATION   2,460.00
INCIDENTAL EXPENSES   245.35

TOTAL EXPENDITURES $9,959.35

BALANCE IN BANK AS OF JULY 1, 1929   94.15

RESPECTFULLY SUBMITTED,

Max Block, Treasurer

THE RADIO APPARATUS

There are in use four amplifiers out of the six that we have and we will not operate the other two until the entire population is confined in the new cell blocks. The number of phone connections and their locations are as follows:

AMPLIFIER 1, FOR LOUD SPEAKERS ONLY—SPEAKERS ARE LOCATED IN THE:

CHAPEL (OLD)	3
HOSPITAL (OLD)	2
CONDEMNED CELLS	3
WARDEN'S HOUSE	2
TOTAL SPEAKERS	10

AMPLIFIER 2, EARPHONES IN OLD CELL BLOCK	587
EARPHONES IN CHAPEL DORMITORY	47
TOTAL EARPHONES ON AMPLIFIER 2	634

AMPLIFIER 3, EARPHONES IN B BLOCK	604
AMPLIFIER 6, EARPHONES IN SEVEN BUILDING	81
EARPHONES IN FIVE BUILDING	285
TOTAL EARPHONES ON AMPLIFIER 6	366

TOTAL EARPHONE CONNECTIONS AS OF JULY 1, 1929   1604

AMPLIFIERS FOUR AND FIVE ARE NOT IN OPERATION

THE AVERAGE DAILY USE OF THE RADIO APPARATUS SINCE ITS INSTALLATION IS FIVE HOURS.

RESPECTFULLY SUBMITTED,
Fisher, League Electrician

STATEMENT SHOWING DAILY AVERAGE OF MOTION PICTURE SHOWINGS AND LEGITIMATE ENTERTAINMENT

Because of the continued changing from the old to the new prison there has been a curtailment of legitimate attractions, with the exception of the Friday evening vaudeville entertainment.

However, with the exception of one or two nights, we have shown a picture in the old chapel every evening and in the new building twice weekly.

The projectors in the old chapel have been used for 456 hours each—and the projector on the hill has been used for 160 hours. By careful and diligent attention being given to these machines, by the operators, we have been able to get the very best results. However, another year will see both machines reduced to such a condition that we will not be able to show a clear and distinct picture and we trust that you will consider this problem when it confronts you.

We realize that there is a possibility of obtaining new material—both stage and booth—when we move to the hill, and because of that fact, we are doing the very best that we can with what we have pending our removal.

Very truly yours,
Charles Dryden,
Director of Entertainment

The work of the Mutual Welfare League is clearly set forth in the above reports. The financial report shows how money is obtained for the various activities. It is commendable of the League that they send money to the families of the inmates so that they can visit their loved ones at the prison. In some instances, the League would help out families in other ways.

Not so long ago, a young wife left two small children at home in her tenement in Brooklyn and came to Sing Sing to see her husband who had been sent up for burglary. They were allowed to see each other in the visiting room, where they talked earnestly until the keeper on duty told them that their time was up. The inmate requested ten more minutes with his wife. The request was granted, but just as the keeper turned his head, the convict plunged a knife into the neck of his wife, severing her jugular vein. The woman fell bleeding to the floor and expired before any assistance could arrive. Where the inmate managed to secure the knife is not known, but it appears to have been slipped under his blouse while he was in the mess hall. He was later sentenced to the chair for this killing. In response, the Mutual Welfare League took up a collection among its members. By adding a bit from their treasury, they were able to send sufficient money to Brooklyn for the provisions of the little ones. An especially sad incident, but one which exemplifies their motto, "Do good and make good."

Better Alive Than Dead

Following the inception of the Mutual Welfare League, Police Lieutenant Charles Becker was electrocuted along with four gunmen for the murder of Herman Rosenthal, a New York gambler. But for the fact that a vaudeville actor had caught the number of the car in which the gunmen sped away from Rosenthal's gambling house on West 45th Street after the murder, the crime might have been added to a growing list of unsolved New York mysteries.

District Attorney Whitman traced the gunmen through the license number of their car and discovered their names—"Gyp the Blood," "Lefty Louie," "Whitey" Lewis, and "Dago" Frank Cirofici. On the strength of their confessions, Lieutenant Becker was indicted and arrested on July 29, 1912. He was put on trial on October 4th. After deliberating for eight hours, the jury decided that Becker was guilty, and he was sentenced to die in the electric chair,

The four gunmen were tried about a month later and convicted on practically the same evidence as in the Becker trial. They were executed in the Sing Sing death house on April 13, 1914. "Dago" Frank made out a confession just before he was taken to the chair in which he stated he had not been engaged in the actual killing. He further said that it was done by the other three and denied that Becker had anything to do with the affair.

Becker's case was taken before the Court of Appeals, which granted him a new trial largely because of their dissatisfaction with the testimony concerning a Harlem conference in which Becker was said to have given orders for the murder of Rosenthal.

The second trial began on May 6, 1914. James Marshall, a Negro and former stool pigeon for the police officer, offered more evidence in support of that given at the original trial. Becker was again found guilty on May 22. The Court of Appeals was satisfied with the trial and upheld his sentence on May 25. An effort was made to place the case before the Supreme Court of the United Sates, but they refused to recognize it.

Becker was taken to the prison immediately after the decision and lodged in the death house until his execution on July 30, 1915. Two priests, in their long robes, walked beside him reading prayers in low voices. I was one of the attendants at the time. I never would have recognized the man as he walked into the fatal chamber. I had always known him as a large, powerful fellow who often headed the strong arm squad in their forays about New York. Now, he seemed shrunken and there was fear in his eyes. He was but a shadow of the man I had known.

Becker issued the following statement just before he was taken to the chair:

Gentlemen: My dying declaration:

I stand before you in my full senses, knowing that no power on earth can save me from the grave that is to receive me. In the face of that, in the teeth of those who condemn me, and in the presence of my God and your God, I proclaim my absolute innocence of the foul crime for which I must die. You are now about to witness my destruction by the State, which is organized to protect the lives of the innocent.

May Almighty God pardon every one who has contributed in any degree to my untimely death. And now, on the brink of my grave, I declare to the world that I am

FIGURE 32. The death chamber takes another man's life. Photo courtesy of the Ossining Historical Society.

proud to have been the husband of the purest, the noblest woman that ever lived—Helen Becker. This acknowledgment is the only legacy I can leave her.

I bid you all good-by. Father, I am ready to go. Amen."[1]

One of Becker's legs was bare from the knee down to the top of his sock. The trouser leg which had been slit down the front was rolled up into a bulge above his knee. There was scarcely a sound save the low voices of the priests as Becker sat down in the chair. The straps were passed across his face, concealing his features. He tried to speak, but just a gurgle came from between those heavy bands across his lips.

The electrician looked at the doctor, waiting for the signal. When it came, his eyes dropped to Becker's chest while he watched the rising and falling of the breathing. Just as the doomed man exhaled, the executioner threw in the switch and I turned away as the straps creaked sharply. It was all over in a few moments. Later, when the doctor performed the autopsy, they found a note on his chest, pinned to the undershirt, saying:

YOU KILLED AN INNOCENT MAN

Shortly after Becker's electrocution, there was an attempted prison escape. The old cell block cells were damp and clammy, thoroughly unfit for men to live in. Due to the uncomfortable conditions, the men were allowed to attend motion pictures every night. This was done to keep them out of the building as much as possible. So, every night at seven, the doors were thrown open to allow those who so desired to attend the show in the chapel. The inmates who did not care to go were again locked in for the night.

On pretense of going to see the performance, three of the inmates left their cells and hid out in the north end of their gallery until the officers had made their rounds, relocking the cells of the men who had remained behind for the night. After this, the guards patrolled the galleries until the return of the men who were in the chapel.

One of the three who hid out acted as a lookout for the other two while they used an automobile jack to pry apart the bars on the small cell block window. This jack had been secreted beforehand in a chosen hiding place. The men had to work very carefully in shifts while the guard was at the far end of their gallery. Only then could they work without the fear of discovery.

A window at the north end of the building had been selected for their escape. A light bulb in this section of the building had been put out of commission during the day and, hence, caused the poorly lit area to be surrounded by shadows. When the guard showed signs of returning to the scene of their labors, the lookout would give the signal and all would return to their hideout until the immediate danger of being discovered had passed. Although unable to see the guard, they could see his shadow silhouetted against the white-washed walls of the cell block. This game of "bar prying" went on until the work was nearly completed. Another moment or so, a pry or two, and all three would have been well on their way to freedom.

However, they did not reckon with fate. As they could see the shadow of the guard against the wall, so could he see theirs when they came out of their retreat to work on the bars at the window.

From where the men were concealed, they had to cross a narrow strip that was fairly well lighted by the glow of the next light. It threw their shadows in sharp contrast against the white-washed background. It was only for a moment, but long enough to catch the trained eye of the guard. At first, he paid little attention to the shadow, thinking it was another officer on his tour of inspection. But it happened repeatedly, and when two shadows appeared simultaneously, the officer thought it time to investigate.

The guard literally sneaked down the corridor, very cautious in his advance. The training to be suspicious of anything unusual he observed, no matter how small it might be, stood him in good stead. His suspicions were verified as he neared the further end of the gallery. Crouching low and well against the cell doors so he would not cast his shadow against the wall, he reached the end of the corridor where the men were quietly working their way out.

The guard waited, scarcely daring to breathe for fear he would reveal his presence. He watched the convicts come from their place of concealment once more and resume work on the bars. They were about fifteen or twenty feet from where the guard crouched. Just when they were about to realize the fruits of their carefully planned getaway, the guard stood up and announced his presence saying, "It's all up, boys. No use making a fuss."

The prisoners realized at once that it would do them no good to put up a fight which would attract the attention of other guards on duty in the hall. Also, there was a heavily armed guard stationed at a post just outside, and they knew he would not hesitate to shoot once an alarm had been given. Though they submitted quietly, they were punished for their pains.

Soon after, we missed a prisoner by the name of Alois Jones. We searched for Jones for fifteen days and nights, but were unable to discover a trace of the man. A few years later, when we were tearing down one of the old prison buildings, we found him dead under the floor. He must have made the compartment, but had been unable to get out after the guards had left and perished in what had become his coffin.

Escapes seemed to run in bunches. Two inmates, Barrett and Stivers, were the next to try their luck. Stivers was in for life, convicted of murdering a policeman. Barrett had been sent up for stealing automobiles. These two men were working in one of the lower offices of the administration building when they initiated their plan. Officer Webster recalled that as he entered the room to count the men, the light was switched off. Almost immediately, he was struck on the head with a sandbag and his revolver, a .38 Colt, was taken from him.

Officer Peter Kagler was their next victim. He was taking a drink of water in the next room when they struck him from behind. He managed, however, to run into the key room and warn Simmons, the officer on duty, before he collapsed. As Simmons stepped into the visiting room, which led to the clerk's office, he was covered with a pistol by Stivers and attacked by Barrett with the sandbag. After a sharp scuffle, the officer was overpowered, and along with Officer Webster, was forced into a big safe. Barrett and Stivers then locked the door and ran to the armory, where they stole a gun just as Kagler came to and gave the alarm. Though the weapon was not loaded, they managed to get through the gates. They stole a car close at hand on Broad Street and rode madly down the river road. Barrett was recaptured a short time after, but nothing was heard of Stivers. He is probably still hiding out somewhere.

I continued working about the prison in various shops including the state shop, wash house, shipping room, and school. It was in the school where I met an inmate who had worked under me some years before. He asked me where all the old keepers were. The man had been away for over thirty years. I replied that most of the old fellows had either died or gone on to something else.

"Well, now, what do you know about that?" said the man. "Did you happen to know a fellow named Conyes? He used to be my keeper. Whatever happened to him anyway?"

"Oh, Conyes," I replied. "Sure, I knew him, but he has been dead for quite some time now. Just what sort of boss was he?"

"I'm telling you," replied the man, "that Mr. Conyes was a hard taskmaster. He certainly made us work, but he wasn't a bad sort, if we did as he told us. I'm sort of sorry to hear that he is gone."

I sent the fellow back to his seat, where he soon learned from the others that the man he was asking about had charge of the room and that he had just finished talking to him.

A few hours later, after the school session for the day, he came up to me and said: "Say, Mr. Conyes, I didn't know you. I'm mighty glad I didn't say anything against you earlier when we were talking. I certainly am glad to see you in such good health. If you ask me, you're still quite a way from the grave."

"Well," said I, "it is a good thing that you didn't say anything bad about me. I'm sorry to see you here again and hope you'll know enough to keep away in the future."

My last regular duty was done on the outside guarding the walls. I was getting pretty well along in years and the work on that post was a bit easier for me. My job was to sit in a tower by the river with a rifle in hand to prevent prisoners from swimming to freedom.

I can recall but one notable occurrence during my time there. It happened while some men were loading a coal barge at the dock. Five of the detail made a break and ran up to the north lookout post, where they overpowered the guard on duty. I saw the whole proceeding from where I sat, but was unable to leave my own post. I picked up the phone and notified the warden. Then, taking my rifle, I aimed at the men who had jumped into the river. I fired a few shots at the leader while the men down below me began to show signs of excitement. I heard one of them saying that I was doing my duty and that they should not make any undue disorder. The first shots from my rifle struck just in front of the leader. I could see the water spurt up where the bullets were striking. I fired a few more, this time a bit closer, but the men kept on. The next shot was placed right

FIGURE 33. Typical watch tower with view of the Hudson River. Photo courtesy of the Ossining Historical Society.

next to the leader's ear. He then threw up his hands as the men below shouted, "He's got him, Mr. Conyes has got him." I hadn't hit the man, however, and they all swam back to the shore, where the guards took them into custody. Later, the warden called me into his office and asked: "Mr. Conyes, did you shoot to kill?"

"No, warden, "I replied, "I shot to bring them back."

This break was practically the last excitement while I was on active duty with the exception of a riot in the mess hall between two prison "political parties." "Vince" Gaffney, who was doing twenty

FIGURE 34. Warden's office. Photo courtesy of Guy Cheli.

years for murder, led the members of the "Tammany" party against James Cleary's "Cheese" party. The two parties had held an election a short time before and the "Tammany" bunch won out. Soon after, Gaffney, who had been transferred to Clinton, returned to Sing Sing and was immediately selected as the "Tammany" leader. His first order was to "razz" the "Cheese" bunch. This was done in the many ways which are never discovered by the keepers or guards. The atmosphere in the cell block became quite tense. Then, one night as the men were filing from chapel through the mess hall after a moving picture, there came a low growl: "Gaffney? Awe, he's a rat."

In an instant, the mess hall was bedlam. Men struck slyly from behind, and many who didn't know what the excitement was all about soon became embroiled in the struggle. Acting P. K. John J. Sheehy and other guards punched their way into the fighting, cursing mob and soon restored order. As a result of the battle, Cleary was put in solitary confinement with a nose nearly severed by a cut from a jagged piece of plate. John McIntyre, one of his aides, occupied another cell with a deep slash across his stomach. Six other participants were also placed in these cells, and although their hurts were painful, they were in no way serious.

A few months after the riot, I was released from active duty and became eligible for a pension, but I had been at Sing Sing for so long, I found it rather hard to give up. Finally, I managed to get the job as official guide, a capacity which I still hold.

The following data was compiled by Warden Lawes after a careful and close survey of the conditions leading to crime.

About 15 per cent of the prisoners give "intoxication" as a cause of their crime, but in view of the fact that a great many men indulge in intoxicants without committing felonies, this cause must not be taken too seriously. It is given, often, to extenuate the criminal act. Note that the prison psychiatrists have found less than 10 per cent actually "alcoholic."

Approximately 30 per cent of the prisoners attribute their crime to "evil companionship" and this appears quite plausible. In fact, this answer ranked first in a questionnaire submitted by the New York State Crime Commission to three thousand prominent men and women. Other causes assigned include need of money, gambling, revenge, drugs, jealousy, and home conditions—the total averaging about 30 per cent. On original commitment, less than ten in a thousand claim a "frame up," and only one in a thousand blames "hounding by the police," though parole violators more frequently make these claims. Claims of self-defense are naturally high in homicide and assault cases.

Innocence is claimed by about 15 per cent of the prisoners. These claims, of course, must be greatly

discounted although it is a fact that a few absolutely
innocent men are sent to prison as a result of mistaken
identity, "frame up," or fortuitous circumstances. Positive
identification has frequently proved erroneous, and men
have been definitely proved to have been innocent after
serving long years in prison.[2]

Sing Sing has quite a few former doughboys within its walls.
They went valiantly "over the top" and plunged headlong into a black
pit of despair. Few, if any, of these soldiers had ever been in prison
before. They all seem to have come by the same road. Practically
all of these unfortunate fellows were honest and law-abiding citizens
before they either enlisted or were drawn into the great conflict by
the draft. Many went away from the wholesome influences of a good
home for the first time. They were like birds first trying their wings,
plunging carelessly to destruction.

Efforts were made to safeguard the morals of these men, but alas
those efforts sometimes failed. Those who had been decent all their
lives fell into bad habits, drinking and gambling—anything to blot
out the horrors of war. Evil associates swooped upon these splendid
young men like hawks and enticed them into various evil ways. Paris
provided the desired outlet. It was so easy to give in to the glamour
and thrill of things in which they were so inexperienced.

When the armistice came, soldiers thought, "Why go home?"
It was such a dead and uninteresting place after their experiences
abroad. The call of the "bright lights" was too strong, and soon, the
poor fellows had lost all of their money. To go home penniless was
impossible. Many men were convicted of highway robbery, some for
snatching packages of money from bank messengers and a few for
homicide. The result was inevitable—prison. Many of the felons in
Sing Sing had been awarded medals for heroism on the battlefield.
Character and self-sacrifice made them heroes, but the war left its
marks. A medal for conspicuous gallantry in action is of little use to
a man in prison.

There can be no doubt that Prohibition, which went into effect
on January 16, 1918, has had an effect on crime. Conditions at the

present time are rapidly becoming worse. Of course, in the days of the saloon, liquor had its effect on those who imbibed, but the buyer was assured of getting the real article for his money. Now, when a man enters a speakeasy, he knows little or nothing as to the quality of the alcohol he buys. He simply takes a chance and very often regrets it. Present day drinking has a devastating effect. Good liquor makes a man drunk, but the liquor sold during Prohibition drives him mad. The enforcement of Prohibition has been very poor to date, and this laxity has created a high disregard for all law. Consequently, the prisons are over-run with men sent up river for all kinds of offenses. "If I can get away with violations of the Prohibition law, why not get away with violations of other laws?" That attitude has a big effect on the potential law-breaker.

However, the true basis for delinquency is the failure of our public schools and social agencies to train our youth for adequate vocations. The lack of proper facilities in our public school system to assist pupils who do not respond to mere book learning causes them to leave school at an early age without any definite means of earning a livelihood. As a result, they drift from one thing to another, and in periods of idleness they are tempted to "run about" in the company of street idlers in back alleys, pool rooms, and places of ill fame.

There are two more factors responsible for the youthful delinquency which leads to crime—the disinterested attitude of the home that fails to supervise the child's leisure moments and the laxity of the church to interest the child in spiritual matters so as to make a better connection between the moral and practical influences.

It has been found that, in neighborhoods where Boy's Clubs and Boy Scout organizations are strong, the delinquency rate has been greatly reduced. In Milwaukee, where the public school system has undertaken official supervision of playgrounds and clubs, the crime rate among its youth has been reduced by more than fifty per cent. In Chicago and other great centers of population, similar results have been obtained. While it is doubtful crime will ever be entirely eliminated, the fact remains that it can be controlled and definitely diminished if our public institutions will conform their programs to social requirements among the children of our large cities. The effectiveness of such responsible programs will have a positive influence upon future generations.

Some men come to prison, work as little as their officers will stand for, spend most idle hours lounging about and go away no better than when they came—in fact worse. The idlers are preyed upon by the more hardened members of their environment and are taught many things they never knew about the ways of criminals. They are the drones in the busy hives of industry found within the walls of Sing Sing. They never make any attempt to draw themselves out of the inertia and will probably continue to remain in it. They are generally the men who come back to serve other terms.

On the other hand, there are inmates who turn their enforced idleness into good account by studying so they may better acquit themselves for honest, useful work when they are released. These men do not loiter around the yard chattering with others. They store away knowledge and try to improve their minds by reading good books. The library is a great privilege to men of this type. There are over twelve thousand volumes to be found here dealing with almost every known branch of literature. Thousands of inmates in the past have bettered themselves simply by the reading done in this building, and many of them now hold good positions in the business world outside of these walls.

Many take up mining and study it until they come out enabled to go far away to obtain good jobs. Some study architecture, some medicine, and others law, while many more take up agriculture resolving to go to the West, to South America and other countries where opportunities await them. Rather than let others know of their past, inmates are generally better off in another country, where they may become respectable citizens without any fear of being ruined by prejudice.

In consideration of the surroundings, my life here has been quite enjoyable, but I doubt if I would ever go through it again. I cannot conceive of a work more weighed down with moral responsibility, for to us are committed, almost body and soul, hundreds of broken, helpless, imprisoned men. Their welfare is in our hands for long, dreary years.

It has been my privilege to bear my share for over half a century in a procession of betterment, a march often halting and always difficult, but nevertheless, constantly upward year by year from the depths of a cold, cruel, and bloody barbarism; up from dungeons, shackles, silence, cages, starvation, the lash, paddle, and club, to the community and honor system of the Mutual Welfare League of today.

Sing Sing, as it is today, is a model penal institution. Great credit is due Warden Lewis E. Lawes for the splendid manner in

FIGURE 35. Sing Sing guards and keepers when Alfred Conyes first worked at Sing Sing Prison—Alfred Conyes, front row, center. Photo courtesy of the Ossining Historical Society.

FIGURE 36. Sing Sing prisoner, chaplain, guards, keepers, and warden. Photo courtesy of the Ossining Historical Society.

which he presides over this community of hardened criminals. He is kind and sympathetic, but at the same time, he is firm and resolute in the discharge of his duties as warden. During my career in the penal institutions of the state, I have served under no less than twenty-four wardens, five of whom are dead, and with all due respect to those men, I regard Warden Lawes as the most capable of all. Warden Lawes is fair and just, and no one can obtain a job through any outside "pull." I am proud to serve under Warden Lawes—the broadest, ablest, most judicially sympathetic and understanding of them all.

I have handled thousands and tens of thousands of criminals from every walk of life and every degree of criminality, but I have never found one that, after he and I understood each other, I need fear for one moment or could not trust.

EDITOR'S NOTE

While editing *Fifty Years in Sing Sing*, I was able to learn a few things about my great-grandfather's life outside of his prison work, about which Ted Conover asked in his foreword—"(Did he have a family? Did he live nearby and walk to work?)."

Alfred Conyes was one of eight children (six boys and two girls) born to Jacob Conyes and Cornelia Osterhoudt. Alfred married Josephine Myer on May 4, 1870, a few weeks shy of his eighteenth birthday. They had a daughter, Lizzie, born July 30, 1872, and a son, Franklin (Frank), born February 22, 1876, Sometime during the next year, 1877, Alfred began his career as a prison officer.

FIGURE 37. Home of Alfred Conyes. Photo from the Conyes family archives.

FIGURE 38. Baby photo of Alfred Stanley Conyes, son of Alfred Conyes, taken before the town changed its name from Sing Sing to Ossining. Photo from the Conyes family archives.

Josephine died on March 5, 1887. Frank died in 1890 at the age of fourteen. Unfortunately, I wasn't able to find further information about Lizzie or the cause of death for Josephine or Frank. Alfred Conyes later married Christina Thornton (date unknown), and they had a son, Alfred Stanley, born June 22, 1892. Their home was on Hamilton Avenue in Ossining, just a half mile from the prison. My grandfather, who went by Stan, married Laura Vosburgh on September 1, 1914. My mother, Laura Virginia Conyes, was born July 11, 1916.

FIGURE 39. Alfred Stanley Conyes, son of Alfred Conyes. Period photos from the Conyes family archives.

FIGURE 40. Alfred and granddaughter Laura Virginia Conyes, August 1918, Ossining, New York. Photo from the Conyes family archives.

Notes

Destiny Carved in Stone

1. Pendleton Act—Civil Service Law, Forty-Seventh Congress of the United States of America, 1883.

Clinton Prison: An Inside Portrait

1. Lawes, Lewis. *Life and Death In Sing Sing* (Garden City, NY: Garden City Publishing Co., 1928).

Sing Sing—Now and Then

1. Lawes.
2. Ibid.
3. Author unkown. Article in *State Service: An Illustrated Monthly Magazine Devoted to the Government of the State of New York and Its Affairs* (Albany: The State Service Magazine Co., Inc., 1922), vol. 6.
4. Lawes.
5. Source unknown.

To Be Put to Death

1. Governor Hill's message to the Legislature, 1885.
2. New York (State) Commission on Capital Punishment. Report of the Commission to Investigate and Report the Most Humane and Practical Method of Carrying into Effect the Sentence of Death in Capital Cases. Transmitted to the Legislature, January 17, 1888. Albany, NY: Troy Press, printers, 1888.
3. *The New York Times*, August 7, 1890.

Holding the Line

1. *The New York Times*, July 7, 1891.
2. Ibid.
3. Ibid.
4. *The New York Times*, July 8, 1891.

The High Cost of Freedom:
Leaving Sing Sing, Leaving This Earth

1. *The New York Times*, March 21, 1893.
2. Ibid.
3. Ibid.
4. *The New York Times*, May 9, 1893.
5. Ibid.
6. Ibid.

A Promise to Be Kept

1. *The New York Times*, February 9, 1898.
2. *The New York Times*, July 13, 1898.
3. *The New York Times*, March 21, 1899.
4. Source unknown.
5. *The New York Herald*, November 29, 1912.

A Narrow Escape, Suicide, and Tragedy

1. *The New York Times*, February 27, 1908.

Do Good and Make Good

1. New York State Prison Commission Report, July 1915.

Better Alive Than Dead

1. *The New York Times*, July 31, 1915.
2. Lawes.

Made in United States
North Haven, CT
03 January 2022

14008480R00114